SCRIPTURE UNION
130 City Road, London EC1V 2NJ

First published 1984
Reprinted June 1986

ISBN 0 86201 233 3

Printed and bound by Cox & Wyman Ltd, Reading

Contents

This book is dedicated
with love
to my two daughters
Gemma and Rhoslyn

1

The stranger from the sky

It was so quiet and peaceful in Mrs. Andrews' classroom that you would hardly believe thirty boys and girls were there, packed quite closely together. There was an atmosphere of concentration in the room. Everyone was doing 'projects', and it was one of those rare times when each member of the class was absorbed in its work. Mrs. Andrews wanted it never to end. She looked up from the page in front of her, her red marking pen held loosely between relaxed fingers. She looked with satisfaction all around the room, savouring the harmony, thinking of the peaceful energy that was being used in the proper way. . . . Beside her, Joanna Gilpin shifted from one foot to the other and fiddled with a piece of hair she had pulled over her shoulder. Mrs. Andrews was recalled to her job of going through Joanna's story. She tightened her grip on her pen and poised it a little way from the page, ready to let it pounce on a mistake. She lowered her eyes to the page. The red pen pounced at once.

'I would like to be a moddle,' Joanna had written. 'I would wear beautiful clothes and be very tall and very thin. . . .'

In the classroom next door, chaos broke out – Mr. Scott's children had come back from their TV lesson in the Hall. Further down the corridor other more distant sounds could be heard. The unrest penetrated into Class A, of course. They shuffled papers softly and began to put lids back on to their felt-tip pens. Over in the corner, Christine David looked up from her page of Vanessids and rested her chin on her hand.

'It must be time for Afternoon Break,' she thought, and felt her heart go lurching towards her bottom rib. Just for a while she had been immersed in a world of butterflies; she had drawn and coloured both the large and small tortoiseshells, and had been wondering where to start on the peacock – the eyes first, or the background?

The noise in the other classroom had disturbed her then. She had been so absorbed that she had forgotten where she was. She had thought she was back in Coryton Primary. Now, as she looked round at the faces of her class-mates, she wished she were two hundred miles away again.

The bell rang, and Class A looked up expectantly, listening to the stampeding next door, and the careless voices as Class B pushed and jostled their way out to the playground.

Mrs. Andrews went carefully and deliberately through another sentence of Joanna's work, though Joanna's eyes strayed furtively around the room. Mrs. Andrews believed in self-control and discipline, and Class A knew it, and that she would only take longer if they packed up before she told them to. They arranged their papers cautiously, with one eye on the teacher's desk. When Mrs. Andrews finally raised her eyes, they were all ready, like thirty coiled springs. She had only to say the word. . . .

She passed Joanna her book, still looking around her class.

'Green Team may go first,' said Mrs. Andrews.

They put their books away, and left in an orderly manner, but once outside, the springs uncoiled, and they were away.

Christine, who was in Yellows, couldn't help feeling expectant. The way Mrs. Andrews set about things tended to make you sit up and listen. Although she dreaded the breaks – Morning, Afternoon and Lunch – she still joined in the coiled spring race, whenever Mrs. Andrews uttered the magic words, 'Yellow Team'.

She couldn't help it. Outside the classroom she found herself joining in, and racing behind Mandy Briggs to the group around Lara. There were three other girls there, and Lara, in her bossy way, was telling them something. For a minute she did not notice Christine, hovering behind Mandy. Then she turned, and at once it all happened again.

'We don't want you – she can't be in this game, can she?' she appealed to the others, who stood like sheep and shook their heads.

'Why not?' Christine asked indignantly, though she had heard it all before, so many times. She felt that lump in her throat coming up again.

'Just because!' snapped Lara, 'So clear off! Go and play somewhere else.'

'Yes, buzz off!' shouted her friend, Fiona. 'We're not having you in our game! You're not wanted, thanks very much!'

'I don't want to be in your silly game!' retorted Christine, and stalked away. No one took pity and came with her. She glanced back over her shoulder when she was a good way off, and saw them getting on with the game as though she didn't exist. They were being joined by the girls from Red and Blue Teams, who had just been let out of the classroom. None of *them* were being turned away by Lara and Fiona. They were busily picking teams it seemed, and Lara and Fiona, with their heads close together, were making chalk marks on the ground.

Christine turned away again. She spotted Sally and Julie playing ball together, and half hopefully wandered up to them.

'Can I play?'

'No. This game is for two.'

They scarcely looked at her. Their games were always for two.

So there it was, in spite of her trying. It had all happened again, and she was on her own again. She walked heavily to the edge of the grass and stood there with her back to the concrete area. She bit her lip hard to try and stop her eyes filling with tears. In front of her the frosty grass was clear of children – the boys all on the other side, the girls all playing on the concrete. Beyond the grass there was a tall hedge, and beyond that, gardens of houses. Christine felt a desperate longing to get out of school somehow. She must get home. She didn't think she could remember the way home because she came to school by car each day. Cars went so fast, and everything looked different when you walked. Still she could try – what did it matter if it took her till tea-time? Nothing mattered except to get home and cry on her mother's shoulder. Thinking of that shoulder nearly made the tears spill right over.

'I won't stay in this horrible school,' she said aloud, 'I hate it here. I want to go back to my old school.'

She stared hard, hard into the wintry sky, trying to make her anger dry up the tears, so that no one should see Christine David of Class A crying alone in the playground. She *would* go home. But it meant walking around the front

– past the Headmaster's window. Or she would have to cross the playground to get to the other gate. She could hardly do that, crying like a baby.

'It's supposed to be a good school,' she said bitterly, aloud again, 'a Church School! Everyone's taught to be kind and to follow Jesus – but they were kinder in my old school. The children there weren't spiteful and unfriendly. I wish we'd never moved to this horrible town.'

A little cloud was in the sky, no bigger than a hand. She stared at it hard, blinking at the tears.

'I've had enough of it,' she said. It was a relief to say it, after eight weeks of misery – trying to make the best of things, pretending they weren't too bad, hoping they would get better.

The cloud was getting bigger. Christine watched it, rubbing her eyes furtively with her thumb while pretending to push ends of hair away from her face, in case anybody should be watching her. The cloud was getting bigger because it was moving, but not going along in the sky the way clouds usually do. It was coming forwards – moving towards the school! She stared at it, fascinated, forgetting her tears. She could hear the shouts of playing children behind her. The cloud was moving very fast. In a few seconds it had come right down on to the grass straight ahead of Christine, just in front of the hedge. The din of the games in the playground behind her did not change; the other children did not seem to have noticed anything odd. But Christine watched – she saw the cloud change – it was taking the shape of a person! Now it was no longer a cloud; it looked like a human being. And it beckoned to Christine.

The noisy games faded behind her, as if the whole playground had moved further away. The grass which had been frosty and greyish, had become a sparkling green. Behind the hedge, the November sky was summer blue. The person from the cloud looked familiar to Christine, though she had no name for him – had she seen him in a dream? What was it about him that made her recognise him? She was quite certain he was not a stranger, and yet she had just seen him come down from the sky! Could he be a Space-man?

He certainly didn't look like Christine's idea of a Space-man. He wore no helmet – his hair was bright and waving. It fell in a fringe across his forehead and it shone as if the sun was shining on it. He wore a clear green tunic – or else the tunic reflected the grass he stood on. When Christine glanced down at his feet she saw that he wore sandals with thongs about his legs, like the Roman soldiers Mrs. Andrews had been teaching them about. His feet were shining! And around his waist he wore a belt which looked like pure gold.

Afterwards Christine remembered all these shining things, and also that there had been a suggestion of shimmering everywhere around him. The light was strange and different where he was. But his face, although she knew it well, she could never afterwards describe. She could only say that he was young, and yet much older than she, and that she would know his face again anywhere. His face was noble, she remembered, and good, and he smiled at her with the smile of a friend. He looked like a human, though Christine had been led to believe that Extra-Terrestrial Beings were all ugly and monstrous, even when they were well-intentioned (which, according to the stories she knew, was not often). But this stranger, who was not a stranger, filled Christine with happiness and comfort, as much as if her father had just walked across the grass into the playground to put her loneliness right for her.

He beckoned again, and Christine ran across the grass. The Man from the Cloud spoke. He had a pleasant voice, with a trace of a foreign accent, 'I am Marturion. I have charge of you – that is why you know me, Christine.'

She stared up at him, wondering what he meant.

'Tell me about your troubles.'

Her misery and anger of a few moments before rushed back into her mind.

'I want to go back to my old school. Mummy said this would be a lovely school. She was sure I'd be happy here. I know it looks very nice and new and all that but it's horrible really – I liked the old place better. I wish we hadn't moved and left all my friends. I just hate it here.'

'It's all right in the classroom,' she went on. 'I like the lessons, and the teachers. But it's the other children. What's the matter with them?'

She knew that he could answer this, somehow. Marturion said, 'They do not welcome strangers into their homes – they have forgotten the old ways of hospitality. If their parents have not taught them how to welcome newcomers, then it is hard for the teachers to put it right. In the playground they go back to their parents' ways.'

'But they should have got used to me by now – it's getting on to the end of term,' said Christine. 'I think Lara and Fiona just hate me – and they won't let the others try to be friendly with me.'

'They are jealous,' said Marturion. 'They are afraid you will become a leader and take all their followers away from them.'

'Well, do you think there's some way I could go back to my old school?' asked Christine hopefully. She felt there was no other answer to such a problem, and looking at Marturion, whose name she had not known a few minutes ago, she felt convinced that he had power to do something about it. It did not occur to her that this was strange.

'Do you want to give up?' he said. 'Don't you know that there is a plan behind this? Why should it be easy, Christine? After all, we are fighting a battle!' As he said these last words he became fierce and happy. Christine was dismayed. She only wanted to go back to Coryton Primary after all.

'I can help you', said Marturion, 'if you are willing to follow the plan of campaign. I have brought something for you. Will you see it?'

'All right – yes, please,' she added, curiously, wondering what he had brought for her, and where he had brought it *from*.

He held out his hand with a plain black bag in it – like a shoe-bag, with a draw-string at the top.

'It is in this ordinary bag so no one will ask questions. Do not, on any account, tell anyone about it – it is for you alone.'

He said this very seriously, but Christine said, 'Yes, but what *is* it, and what do I do with it?'

Marturion laughed joyfully. 'It is an Eye of Time and Space,' he said, as if she knew all about such things. 'I am allowed to lend it to you for a little while. It is very precious and must be kept secret.'

Christine took the bag gingerly, forgetting about saying thank you. It was not very heavy. Marturion went on, 'In the bag is a small box. Be careful with it – it is very special, very beautiful. You may open the lid whenever you want to, as long as you are quite alone. Farewell, Christine – remember to keep it secret.'

As he said the last words Christine had the sensation that she was on a moving platform and was going away from him.

'Oh, don't go,' she cried – although it was her that was going!

'We will meet again.'

His voice came out of the distance. There was nothing there but a distant cloud, and Christine was standing on the edge of the playground watching it. She had lost that sinking feeling while she had been talking to Marturion, and she still felt better, more like the old happy-go-lucky Christine David of Coryton Primary days. She noticed again the noises of the playground and heard the bell ringing for the end of Afternoon Break. And she turned in amazement, for once again she had fogotten that she was in St. Mary's. The other children were running to get into their lines in front of the teacher who was ringing the bell. No one was looking Christine's way. No one had seen the mysterious Cloud Person who had been there, right in their own school grounds, talking to Christine David over by the hedge.

2

The box

Christine felt bemused and unreal. She walked slowly towards her line, glancing back once or twice at the grass, and the hedge, and the backs of the houses, which appeared just as usual again. Then, as she moved into the line, something bumped against her leg. It was the bag she had been given, swinging from its string in her hand. It had not been a dream – the meeting with Marturion – it had been real. And now she had this strange box-thing to prove it to herself.

She longed to look at the box, but there was no chance. The rest of the day passed in lessons and storytime. Christine drew boxes all through storytime. What did such a thing as an Eye of Time and Space look like? She drew an eye on the last box.

As soon as school was over, she seized the pretend shoe-bag and was first out of the cloakroom, her coat flapping in the chilly wind, her gloves stuffed into her pockets. Her mother, waiting at the gate, sighed when she saw her coming. Christine was such a nice-looking girl, when she was tidied up. She had a lovely oval face, and her hair, when it was well brushed, was a rich shining brown with golden lights. But mostly she looked like a female tramp, or a scarecrow, with everything flapping about or falling off. Her mother noticed too, that she ran out of school alone, while the other children mostly came out in groups, talking eagerly all at once, or running races. Christine had had plenty of friends at her old school, Mrs. David thought. She was good-natured and lively. In Mrs. David's experience, children simply didn't notice untidiness. Christine was clean, and she had the right uniform. Mrs. David worried to herself – what was wrong?

Anne, her younger daughter, was hugging her sister – *she* was quite happy and popular down at the Infants' end of the school. They set off to the car. Anne said, 'What've you got your shoe-bag for, Kissy?' but at the same time Mrs. David said, 'Ballet tonight – we must hurry and have tea.' So the question wasn't answered. Christine loved ballet, but for the first time she thought 'Bother!' and looked ruefully down at the shoe-bag. There was no spare time on dancing nights, and this one was no exception. It was worse than usual as an exam was coming up, and there were some extra details to be sorted out after the class. When they got home it was so late that Anne was going to bed the same time as Christine. She was excited about this and kept running in and out of her sister's bedroom. When the lights were finally out and Anne had stopped singing in the dark next door, Christine was already asleep and knew no more, till her mother in desperation to get her up, pulled the duvet off her at a quarter to eight the next morning.

When she was cleaning her teeth after breakfast, Christine remembered the Eye of Time and Space! They were late. Her father was already in the car, warming the engine. Mrs. David was helping Anne to put her gloves on. 'Come on, Kissy!' Anne was shouting. Christine dashed into the bedroom and pulled the shoe-bag out from under the bed. There would be a lonely playtime, she thought grimly, when she would be able to look at it.

When the bell rang half-way through the morning, her heart filled with excitement and she rushed into the cloakroom as soon as Mrs. Andrews had called 'Yellows'. She let the others run on out into the playground ahead of her this time and lingered by her peg till they'd gone. Someone, to her great irritation, came up behind her and pulled her pony tail. It was Lara, grinning nastily, 'You needn't try to come and play with us – because you can't!'

'I can't think why anyone wants to play with *you*!' retorted Christine, d by her, taking the bag off her peg as she did so. Its touch comforted her and she felt as if Marturion was nearby. 'Well, I've one friend,' she thought. 'He really cared about me. He came specially to bring me this, and now at last I'm going to get a chance to look at it. But *you'll* never have such a thing, Lara – and none of you'll ever know about it.' Satisfied with her secret, she tucked the bag under her coat and went out.

A playground is a very public place, even if no one wants to play with you. Christine hesitated. 'He said it was to be a secret – where can I go to look at it?' She wandered towards the hedge – the place where she had seen Marturion the day before. Today the sky was stormy and grey. She noticed a gap in the hedge to her right, where a large tree grew. She looked round to see if anyone was watching, then stepped quickly through the gap and got behind the tree. Now she could see a space right in the middle of the hedge. She squeezed herself into it and peeped out between the branches and leaves. Some way off children were running about and shouting, but no one was near the hedge, and no one had noticed her. This was a perfect place. There was even a bit of dead branch to sit on. For the first time since she had come to her new school

Christine felt happy alone at playtime. She opened the bag.

The little box was so beautiful. 'It's just as he said – it's precious,' she thought, as she held it on the palm of her hand, looking at it in wonder. It seemed to be made of some kind of stone. Perhaps it was alabaster. It was white, with a touch of pink, and there was a curious and lovely design on the lid in blue, rose and gold. Christine stared at it for a while, thinking that she would like to draw it.

'An alabaster box,' she thought. She had heard that somewhere, and it sounded beautiful. 'Now,' she thought, 'I'll look inside.' Slowly, she opened the lid, holding her breath.

It was lined with blue shiny material, but there was nothing else in it. The lining was lovely to look at – it reminded Christine of twilight after a sunny day when the sky is still wonderfully blue, just about to deepen and fade into navy, then inky black. Christine forgot her disappointment at finding the box empty. As she gazed at the blue which didn't fade, a sparkle appeared in it, like one tiny diamond. It grew larger – it was spinning. Larger and larger it grew, still spinning; then Christine forgot about the alabaster box, and the blue of its lining and everything except the spinning diamond which had become very large, so large that it was blotting out the hedge. It slowed and stopped spinning, and Christine saw a doorway in front of her. Beyond it she could see a greenish-brown area stretching away and away, a vast distance, and, dimly, near the top of the doorway, she could see something glaringly bright.

The next minute she was standing right in the doorway, looking out over what appeared to be a vast grassland, with scrubby bushes here and there, and a hot, hot sun beating down on her.

3

The boy in the pit

A few yards in front of the doorway there was a great hole in the ground, which seemed to be lined with rock. Christine could hear a strange sound coming from it – a sort of hoarse, gasping sound. Then an odd thing happened to her. Inside her head she heard the words, 'Help me!' Then again, 'Oh, who will help me?' The words came quite clearly into her mind. She looked all around her, and there was nobody to be seen in this hot dry-looking place. But up in the dazzling sky, a cloud appeared.

'Oh, could it be Marturion?' she thought hopefully.

The cloud was getting nearer – it was coming down, just as it had before. Christine held her breath – and then, just as before, and just as silently, the cloud came down, touching the earth at the edge of the rocky pit, and Marturion was there.

'Oh, Marturion!' Christine ran up to him, delighted, but he was looking intently into the great hole. She stood beside him and peered down. It was not as dark as she had expected, because the sun was so high overhead and the rocky sides of the pit so straight that there was very little shade even down there. It went down about twenty feet and was dried up and dusty at the bottom. There was one bit of shade cast by a rock jutting out near the top.

Huddled in this shadow was a young man. The hoarse gasping sound came from him. He wore sandals with leather thongs and a cream-coloured tunic which left his arms bare. He seemed to have clasped his arms around his head, and lay face downwards on the baked earth.

'Oh – he's fallen,' cried Christine, 'How can we get him out?' she asked Marturion, but she kept one eye on the boy in the pit, expecting to see him look up at the sound of her voice. But he remained huddled in the shade just as before, oblivious of the presence of two rescuers. Yet again, she found the words, 'Help me, God' coming into her mind. She looked at Marturion.

'Is he unconscious? Perhaps he hit his head when he fell down there.'

Marturion shook his head.

'He is conscious – just. But he is thirsty – he has no water down there.'

Without any warning he stepped off the edge into the hole, and as Christine gasped she saw him land lightly at the bottom of the pit beside the boy on the ground. The boy did not move or look up. Marturion laid his hand on the boy's head, and the boy gave a sort of a sigh, and though he did not really move, Christine thought that he relaxed. Marturion sprang up out of the hole again. He smiled gently at Christine's gaping face and said, 'I have done what I could for him.'

Christine had felt that Marturion was a wonderful and powerful being, from the moment she had first seen him, although he looked so young. Now she felt dismayed that he did not seem able to do much at all.

'Couldn't – couldn't you have lifted him up and jumped up here with him?' she faltered.

'I could touch him,' said Marturion. 'I am not allowed

to do more. He will forget his sorrows for a while, and sleep. And he will dream of comfort and hope. He will awake refreshed.'

Christine felt that more practical help was needed. When the boy woke up he was going to be just as badly off as before. She started to say, 'But dreams aren't much good – he's still stuck down there.'

But Marturion smiled and said, 'Be patient, Christine,' and he touched her arm. She found that she was standing beside him in the doorway made by the Eye of Time and Space. Now she saw that a group of men was coming towards the pit, and she felt relieved.

'Oh, I *see*,' she whispered, but Marturion smiled at her in an amused and tolerant way – like a grown-up. He said, 'Listen carefully, and you will be able to hear them.'

Christine was well able to hear them because they were making such a din. There were about ten of them and they were dressed like the Arabs she had seen on television. They were all talking and shouting and arguing and none of them was listening. As they got nearer, Christine began to doubt whether they would be any use at all as rescuers for the boy in the pit, and the nearer they got the more unsuitable she decided they were. Their faces were full of fury, and passion, their white teeth flashed behind their black beards, and their eyes rolled wildly in their dark skin. Christine was really frightened when they reached the pit, and shrank back. Then she heard Marturion's calm voice saying clearly, 'Don't be afraid. They are unable to see us. We are outside their time and place.'

She found it difficult to believe this as they were only a few feet away from her, but it was true that they took absolutely no notice of her or of Marturion. They seemed quite well aware of the pit, however. They all stopped about a foot from the edge, without even looking at it, as if they knew the place only too well.

Now Christine began to understand what Marturion had meant when he had said that she must listen carefully so as to be able to hear them. At first, their voices were loud and harsh, but the sounds they were making were just babble to Christine, and she realised they were speaking in a foreign language. But as she listened, a phrase came into her mind here and there, as though somebody was translating for her over a little radio.

'He's had enough now – you don't really want to kill him – '

'We certainly do – '

'Let's be done with the dreamer!'

'No one will ever know what's happened to him – '

'We can say we never even saw him!'

'We'll move the flocks tomorrow – '

Christine supposed that even if the boy in the pit woke up and bellowed for help at the top of his voice, he'd never be heard through their noise. The one who looked like the oldest seemed the most reasonable. He seemed to be trying to calm the others down, only he had to shout to be heard. He was rather like a referee, surrounded by a crowd of angry football players, Christine thought. One of the 'players' had a robe over his arm which he waved in the 'referee's' face in an angry and threatening way, and pointed to or shook. The others all seemed to be fussing about this garment too, and she saw that it was a much finer affair than anything the others were wearing. It was richly decorated with many colours, whereas their clothes were made of rough woollen material, in what Christine's mother would have called 'natural' shades. Christine looked at Marturion.

'Oh dear,' she whispered, 'I think I understand now. That boy down there in the pit is a rich nobleman's son, or maybe a prince, even. And these men are bandits who've waylaid him and taken his things – and they're talking about murdering him. Oh Marturion, surely you can do something!'

In an instant Marturion had gone from her side and was standing beside the oldest man who seemed to be losing the argument. He did not see Marturion beside him, but he suddenly spoke with a firm clear voice and was heard over all the others.

'We will leave this now – it is time to eat. We will speak of it afterwards.'

The other men became almost docile; at any rate they seemed satisfied with this arrangement. They all moved away to where Christine could see some tents among the trees, and Marturion came back to her side.

'Do you know who these are?'

'They're robbers and murderers, aren't they?' said Christine. 'They've got such horrible faces – I'm glad they can't see us. I feel so sorry for that poor boy. Can't we do something for him now?'

'They are all his brothers,' said Marturion, gesturing towards the young man in the pit, who seemed to have slept soundly through all the din. He smiled almost mischievously at Christine's astounded face.

'Brothers!' she said, and stopped.

'Yes, brothers. They are not your idea of brothers?' Marturion's smile was a sad one this time, and he shrugged, 'It is surprising how much hatred can come into families, if everyone is not careful. There is a lot of jealousy in this one – did you see his coat, for instance? Quite different from theirs! He has been made the favourite and set above them. He acts like a young lord. He has dreams of lording it over his brothers, and he tells them! They detest him.'

Christine began to feel less sorry for the young man in the pit now. There was something familiar about this story too. It was like one she had heard before.

'It's all got too much for them,' Marturion was saying. 'They won't put up with him any more. They are fine young men, too – sons for a father to be proud of. But this is what jealousy has brought them to. Later on they will bitterly regret it, when they see what they have done to their father.'

'Will they murder him then? And what is going to happen to them all?' asked Christine. She began to see the problem. Even if Marturion rescued the young man now, it would not solve it. It would not cure the brothers' jealousy, or the problem about him being the favourite son.

Marturion was standing with his arms folded looking over towards the tents.

'Their jealousy has reached murder point,' he said. 'A deadly sin. But I am sent to deliver them from it.'

Christine looked at him curiously. How could you deliver people from a deadly sin? Stop them from doing it, she supposed. But wouldn't they do it next time they had the chance? Would you have to keep on watching them, and stopping them?

'The boy in the pit . . .' mused Marturion as if he were talking to himself, 'he has so many gifts – but such a lot to learn . . . chiefly humility and endurance . . . and of course, the chance of an education is not to be turned down. . . . Well, we shall see. After all, he called to my Lord for help. . . .'

While Marturion had been thinking aloud like this, and Christine had been listening, and trying to understand, time had moved on in the grasslands. The sun was less high, and Christine noticed the shadows of the little trees and the rocks. Then she noticed something happening over at the tents of the brothers. There were camels grazing. Perhaps there was a well or a pool there, for she saw men bringing waterskins and loading them on to the camels as if they had been newly filled. These men were strangers, but soon she saw some of the brothers coming towards the pit again. One had a rope, another a waterskin.

'Oh, I think they're going to get him out now!' she said to Marturion in alarm, 'They won't murder him, will they? Have they calmed down?'

'Oh yes,' said Marturion, 'They're quite a lot calmer now they've had their dinner. They've thought of a plan for getting rid of him once and for all, and for doing themselves a bit of extra good.'

He smiled as he stood watching, still with his arms folded on his chest, and Christine moved close to him, half frightened at what she would see. Yet Marturion was not alarmed, so it must be all right.

The brothers came to the pit and dangled the rope into it, roaring abuse. Then they began to heave and soon the boy came over the edge, struggling and panting. He stood up and lifted his arms, which were tied together, and began to rub his face with his forearm. One of the brothers put the waterskin in his hands. He looked so hot and red, Christine was glad to see him take a long drink and splash the water over his face, before they pushed and jostled him over towards the tents.

Coming towards them were the rest of the brothers and

two strangers. But the oldest brother, the one who had been the 'referee', was not anywhere to be seen. The one who held the rich-looking coat was now the leader. He was talking to a little tough-looking man, with crooked legs, and a filthy band round his head. When they reached the group from the pit, the brothers made a circle round the hated 'favourite' while the strangers walked around him, and prodded him and felt his arms and legs, like dealers looking at a horse. The young man was weak, after his day in the pit without food or water, but he stood proudly and glared at the strangers in a haughty and disdainful way. Christine felt very sorry for him again, as he stood there with his hands tied, surrounded by people who hated him. She glanced at Marturion, but *he* was looking quite pleased with everything.

The dealer began counting coins into the hand of the chief brother, most of the others crowding round to look. The boy stood alone; Christine wasn't sure if he was not crying. One of the strangers gave him another drink then, and the boy tilted his head back and drank, tears running down his face.

Then Christine saw that Marturion was standing beside him talking to him. The little toothless man came away from the group, and, not taking a bit of notice of Marturion, seized the rope at the prisoner's wrist and walked away. The boy lifted his head up and turned his back on his brothers, very determinedly. He walked willingly towards the camels with the dealer. He looked tall and straight.

Marturion was standing beside Christine again. He said, 'They have sold him to be a slave. Now he will have to trudge behind the camels all the way to Egypt. Then he will work for the foreigners with no pay.'

'I think he looks more like a prince than a slave,' said Christine, thoughtfully, 'What did you say to him?'

'I told him all will work out for good. I told him all his dreams were right. If he keeps faith they will come true. It will be all right – he can learn much in Egypt. It is in fact, quite a good chance for him!'

Marturion smiled at Christine, and put his hand over her hand, as if closing something up in her palm.

Christine felt cold, as if the sky had darkened and a chill wind had suddenly blown over her. Far off she heard a bell. Then she saw that she was surrounded by the bare twigs of a hedge, and was sitting on a tree trunk, with the lovely alabaster box, shut, on the palm of her hand. . . . She put it back in the bag and squeezed out of her hiding-place. There was no sign of Marturion. But as she walked across the grass to her line, she could still hear his ringing voice: 'He can learn much in Egypt.'

Nobody in the line took any notice of her. She might still have been outside their time and place. They were all arguing and bickering among themselves.

'I touched you, Sam – you weren't over the line!'

'No you never. I *was* there wasn't I, Nicola?'

'No you weren't!'

'Yes she was!'

'No! I touched her!'

'They sound like that gang of brothers,' thought Christine. She couldn't help smiling. She saw that Joanna Gilpin was looking at her.

'Silly, aren't they?' said Joanna, as the line moved off towards the door to the cloakrooms. The argument had subsided into a hissing and glaring match between Nicola and Fiona, as the line went into the school. But Christine and Joanna were grinning together.

4

Ups and downs

The next day was very wet so nobody was able to go outside, and, as it happened, Christine had quite a happy day. She and Joanna volunteered to go down to the Infants' part of the school to help keep them amused during play-times. Christine enjoyed being Anne's big sister and feeling admired. And she wondered if, perhaps, Joanna Gilpin might become her friend.

That afternoon, she made an interesting discovery. It was like this. Mr. Roberts, the curate of St. Mary's, came to give Class A their weekly Scripture lesson. This week he started on the story of Joseph. And almost at once Christine realised that it was part of this story that she'd witnessed the day before! Of course it had never dawned on her before that the Eye of Time and Space had taken her back so many thousands of years – right back to what people call 'Bible times'. She felt so excited about the discovery that she was almost going to put up her hand to tell Mr. Roberts that she had seen that famous coat of many colours. She longed to describe it to the class. She couldn't imagine why she hadn't known at once that it was Joseph who had been down there in the pit and his eleven brothers who had been carrying on like angry footballers! But then, of course she had not known what would happen when she opened the alabaster box – she had not even known what an Eye of Time and Space was.

While she was sitting there in a whirl of thoughts, Mr. Roberts was still talking, and gradually Christine began to listen again. He was asking the class to write the story in their own words, with drawings, if they liked. He was going further. He was offering a prize of a large bar of the best chocolate for the story he liked best.

Naturally everyone was willing to have a try. They had all been taken to see 'Joseph and the Amazing Technicolour Dreamcoat', which had been performed by one of the Secondary Schools last term – (except Christine, who had not been at St. Mary's then). But this, of course, didn't bother her. She took a large sheet of paper and started, trying to remember everything she had seen and heard with Marturion the day before. It was a wonderful chance to tell what she knew, without giving away the secret of the box. Her pencil flew over the paper. She took another sheet. When she got to the part of the story she hadn't observed she found she could make it up quite well, from her memory of the Bible story. She remembered Marturion's words, 'He can learn much in Egypt', and thought about them. Joseph had had a fairly successful time, then a set-back. He had been thrown into prison, quite unfairly. 'What could you learn in prison?' wondered Christine, fiddling with her pencil. Marturion had used some long words – humility and endurance, wasn't it? She supposed prison was a good place for that. In the end he had got out and become a great ruler. His brothers had come and bowed down to him, begging for corn. He had forgiven them, and all had come right. They had all become better people by the end of the story, thought Christine, and her pencil began to fly over the paper again. She just managed to write the last sentence as the bell went for the end of the afternoon.

The next day was also wet, and a happy one for Christine. When they had Art, Mrs. Andrews suggested that they do a pattern or design, and she knew at once that this was her chance to try to draw the pattern on the alabaster box. She worked and worked, felt she couldn't get it right, and was sitting looking at it despairingly when Mrs. Andrews came round and exclaimed, 'That's really lovely, Christine. I'll pin that up on the display board.' Although she knew she had not been able to achieve the design she had wanted, Christine felt proud and happy, and left school that afternoon feeling contented, for the first time since she had been at St. Mary's.

The next day, she arrived feeling cheerful and prepared for a nice day. When she reached the classroom the first thing she looked at was her design. It had been ripped nearly in two, as if someone had been going to tear it down and had stopped short for some reason. Lara and Samantha were standing near the board.

'Who did this to my picture?' Christine asked them, furiously.

Samantha looked quickly at Lara, who shrugged, 'Why should we care what happens to your stupid picture?' she said.

One of the boys, Ian, was sorting out his desk. He said, without looking up, 'She knows who did it. She did it herself.'

'I did not!' yelled Lara, running at him and starting to thump him with her fists. Ian at first shielded himself with his arms, then unfortunately for him, began to thump back, just as Mrs. Andrews came in. He and Lara both got extra work, to be done during playtime, and the whole class got a lecture on how the top class ought to behave.

Christine showed Mrs. Andrews her torn picture, though she didn't say that that was what the two had been fighting about, nor that she thought Lara had done it. The whole class then got another lecture about not touching the display board, and the day started in a subdued manner.

It improved for Christine, at least, as it went on. During Morning Break, the girls wanted to play rounders, and as Lara was not there to take the lead, they let Christine join in, in spite of Fiona's sulky looks. In the afternoon, when she had finished her English exercise, Mrs. Andrews let her start her box design all over again to replace the one which had been spoilt. She even let her stay in during Break to finish it. When it was done, Christine felt it was better than the first one. Mrs. Andrews pinned it on the board and it was admired by several people.

By the following Monday, Christine had almost forgotten she had had troubles at school. She ran off gaily into the playground, waving to her mother. Mrs. David felt relieved.

'Maybe she's settled down at last,' she thought, 'she seems to be happier, thank goodness.'

But at playtime the whole wretched business began all over again. When Christine ran out with the others to the rounders group, Lara turned on her at once. 'Buzz off!' she said, 'You can't play – we've got enough.'

'I *can* play, can't I?' said Christine appealing to the others.

They were all silent – some looked away. Fiona said quickly, 'We've got enough. You'll make it uneven.'

'We only need five a side,' said Samantha. 'We can't have five on one side and six on the other – that wouldn't be fair.'

'Well, let someone else drop out then,' said Christine. 'Toss a coin for it – *that* would be fair.'

'We haven't got a coin – ' Fiona started, but Lara interrupted her.

'Come on – we don't want to stand here all day!' She walked away, tossing the ball from hand to hand, and Mandy Briggs followed her with the bat.

'You're on my side, Fiona,' shouted Lara, and Fiona went over to them. The others drifted after her. Christine watched them picking their teams. She felt as if she might burst. For one raging moment she thought of getting in their way and spoiling the game – tripping the runners up, snatching the ball and throwing it over the hedge into the gardens. . . . But she was not spiteful, although she truly hated them all at that moment. Her commonsense told her that they would only gang up on her the more, and she might be reported to Mrs. Andrews and get into more trouble.

There seemed to be no escape from her misery, and yet again, the longing to be back at her old school overcame her. How could she belong here among these awful children? Some of them might have been nice, but they let that horrible Lara be their leader.

Then she remembered the Eye of Time and Space, and bit her lip crossly. Because things had been so much pleasanter, she had not brought it to school with her that morning. She realised that she was not sure where it was at home, even. She went and sat down on the grass and stared gloomily at the rounders game from a distance. Her mother was always telling her how careless and untidy she was – what if she had lost the Eye of Time and Space? She felt panic tightening up inside her. Then suddenly it all became unreal, and she wondered if she had dreamt it after all. She made a resolution that as soon as she got home she would tidy her bedroom, and would put the pretend shoe-bag somewhere safe. She would try to be more orderly from now on. In fact she would tidy up the mess in her desk too. She felt more cheerful, as she made these plans, almost forgetting that she was sitting by herself.

Suddenly she heard a thwack and saw the ball coming straight towards her, over the grass. Lara had made a very good hit, and Joanna was puffing along after it. It was touch and go as to whether Lara would make a rounder. Christine, getting ready to stop the ball, did not notice this. An idea came to her – if she threw the ball in the wrong direction, Joanna would have to run still further. Joanna was on the plump side and not too good at running; it would pay her back for not taking her side, thought Christine. She had thought Joanna was a bit friendlier towards her than the other girls – but today Joanna had joined with them again.

At that moment a couple of boys came tearing across the grass. They ran in front of Joanna just as the ball reached Christine. She caught it, and then, on the spur of the moment, slipped it under her pleated skirt, which was spread out on the grass. The boys went by, Christine was sitting just as before, staring into space, and Joanna was looking about her in a puzzled way. She stopped by Christine.

'Did you see the ball?'

Christine pretended not to know she was being spoken to.

'Christine, where did the ball go? Did you see it?'

'I expect those boys kicked it,' said Christine. 'It went right under their feet, didn't it?'

Joanna wandered about, looking puzzled, and Mandy ran up shouting crossly, 'Oh come on, Joanna, Lara's made a rounder!'

Christine stopped gloating to herself and felt dissatisfied, because after all she had not meant to help Lara make a rounder. Just then the bell went. Everybody started running to the lines but Mandy and Joanna stayed near Christine looking for the ball. Now she was in a dilemma. She couldn't go on sitting there, but how could she stand up and still conceal the ball? Wishing she hadn't given in to that mean impulse, she got to her feet slowly, turning over on to her knees with her back to the other girls, and wriggling the ball under her cardigan. Then she strolled over to the line, not looking back, and stood behind a group of boys. Mandy and Joanna came running up, looking hot and bothered, and the line moved off.

'You took our ball didn't you, Christine?' said Mandy, and Christine stuck her nose in the air and retorted, 'Why should I look after your ball for you? I hope you've lost it – serves you right!'

Now she had told a lie – or as good as – but she kept telling herself that she had not actually said she *hadn't* taken the ball. She rushed into the girls' toilet and shut herself into a cubicle. There was nowhere she could hide the ball. She pushed it further up under her armpit and came out. Mandy was outside, watching her suspiciously and immediately went into the cubicle where Christine had been, thinking she had put the ball down somewhere. Christine looked about the wash-room wildly – ah, the window was open a little way! She ran the taps as if washing her hands, and glanced over her shoulder to see if Mandy had come out yet. Then she dropped the ball out of the window, where it fell with a soft thud among the dustbins. Christine just got her hands under the tap as Mandy came out. She felt uncomfortable and angry, but relieved that she had got rid of the wretched ball. She didn't like being mean, and she went back into the classroom, wondering why the others had to be so horrible and force her into it.

5

Strange ways of travelling

She shook off the memory of the whole business and stuck to her plan of tidying her desk. Then when she got home she went off by herself and started to tidy her room. Anne was playing with Harriet from next door and Mrs. David was cooking the evening meal.

Christine started with her bed, which looked as if a small earthquake had taken place in that area. She cleared everything off it, shook up the duvet and tried to make it look the way her mother managed to do it. She felt rather pleased with the result. She had arranged her large toy Panda on the pillow with the Pierrot doll she had had for her last birthday beside him. The duvet and the pillow-case were green, and the two magical-looking creatures sat there on the green hill of the pillow gazing at her in a friendly sort of way. Christine stood admiring it all and making resolutions to make it look like this every day. Then she stepped backwards a bit and felt something go crunch – she had trodden on a ball-point pen on the floor, half-hidden among the litter. She made a bit of space on the floor by pushing some of the things aside, got down on her elbows and knees and began to fish under the bed. Her mother was always complaining about the things she kept under the bed. She pulled out two socks (from different pairs and both dirty); a half-finished jig-saw, one odd page from *Reader's Digest*, two crumpled World Wildlife Fund posters, one leg (dismembered from her old teddy bear), one piece of Christmas wrapping paper (from last Christmas), one small knitted toy (belonging to Anne actually), one odd bedroom slipper, one hanky, several oddments of paper and a pixie off a perfume bottle. There were also no less than seventeen books (not together, in a pile, but spread about here and there). By the time she'd been on her stomach for some time pulling all these things out on to the floor beside the bed, she felt like having a break.

She sat up and took a deep breath – then she saw it. Down between the bed and the bedside table a piece of black cord stuck out. She pulled carefully and out came the black bag. One of her mother's favourite sayings was that you would find everything you'd lost if you just tidied up. Christine had never experimented with it before. She held the little bag tenderly to her with a relieved sigh. She vowed that when she had tidied her room this time she would keep it so that it was absolutely perfect. None of her treasures would ever get lost again. But before she cleared up the rest of the room she would just take a peep at the box. . . .

She opened the bag. The box looked different! She drew it out, frowning. Either it was not *the* box, or it had changed. It was quite different, though the same size. This one was a deep, blue grey with a kind of mother-of-pearl design on the lid. She felt again in the bag, in case the first box was still there. She examined the bag – there was nothing else in it, and the bag was exactly as before. Could someone have changed the boxes? It seemed ridiculous to imagine that. She stared at the new box – it was beautiful too – but more severely beautiful.

She decided to open it – it would prove whether it had anything to do with Marturion at any rate. She lifted the lid. . . .

At once she was turning over and over and falling, in complete darkness. She didn't know which way up she was. Something was throwing her about. It felt like a roller-coaster. But why was it so dark, so frightening? She could not shut the box, she seemed to have no control over her body – she was falling, swooping down very fast – now she was travelling upwards and sideways. She wanted to hold her head, to call out 'Stop it'. Suddenly, with a jerk, she was falling again, as if she had gone over some fearsome edge. She tried to get her breath and heard her own terrified voice gasping 'Help! Help!'

She began to rise again and opened her eyes – she had shut them tightly the moment she began to fall. It was dark, but she could make out some shapes in the darkness. Something dark, huge and heavy went rushing past just below her. She was so frightened that she instinctively leaned away from it and her hand touched something hard beside her. As the falling feeling began again she grabbed at the hard thing with both hands and found that she was clasping something that felt like a wooden telegraph pole. She now realised she was sitting on something hard, but the falling sensation was making her so dizzy that she could do nothing but clutch the pole tightly. Her head was bent, her cheek pressed against the pole. She realised there was something – some *things* moving below her – quite a long way below. And the din, the voices were coming from below too. Now she could make out people, staggering about far away beneath her.

Suddenly there was a smell of the sea – Christine knew it well. That smell was the one nice thing in this frightening adventure. But what was it doing here? Now she was moving upwards again, and her pole was going with her!

While she had been falling, Christine could think of nothing, but when she began to move upwards again, it suddenly dawned on her that she was on a ship.

'I'm somewhere up near the top of the mast! There are people down on the deck – and that white thing is a wave. Oh look out, here's another one!'

This time she felt the cold spray and gasped. There was a good deal of yelling and shouting going on below.

'Those people on deck must be soaked,' thought Christine. Just then the huge flapping thing rushed by below her and there was a terrific jerk that nearly threw Christine from her hold on the mast. Even as she thought, 'There goes the sail!' she heard the frantic voices below, and made out one which cried, 'We're sinking!'

Christine felt a great fear surging like a wave through her chest. The ship seemed to be leaning over so far. She felt her head spinning. She heard herself moan, 'Oh, where am I? Oh, save me, someone!'

A clear voice said, 'You are with me again.'

Christine recognised the voice.

'Marturion! I can't see you!' she gasped (with her eyes still tightly shut).

'Hold on,' said his voice. 'Hold on to me and come.'

She felt a touch on her arm but she was scared to let go of the mast. She waited in vain for the ship to steady itself.

'Reach out,' said Marturion's voice again. 'Don't be afraid.'

For a moment she was afraid, then she trusted him, and took one hand off the mast. At once a hand came into her hand and she felt herself lifted up so that she was floating in the air beside Marturion. She could see him now. He glimmered in the half dark. Christine remembered once seeing waves sparkling in the dark, when she had gone for a walk along the beach with her father when they were on holiday. Phosphorescence, her father had called it. She stared at Marturion in wonder, forgetting all about the ship and the storm. She still felt dizzy, the way you do when you've come off a rather fast fair-ground ride.

As the dizziness wore off she ventured to look down. The poor little ship was still plunging about in the waves below them. The deck was running with water and a group of men was struggling across it. They stopped at the rail. Then she heard a cry, – a despairing wail, 'Now! And may your God have pity on us!'

She heard the words distinctly, and at the same time she saw a dark figure fall from the ship into the sea.

'Oh no!' she cried. 'Someone's fallen in!'

No one was throwing a line to him. Just for a moment she saw his head bobbing, then a wave broke over it and over the ship. After that there was no sign of the man.

'Marturion!' cried Christine, 'This is awful! Why did I have to come here! It's terrible. I can't stand it. Don't let's stay and see the ship sink. Oh *please* let's go home!'

Marturion looked at her, and as she looked into his bright face the sky seemed to lighten behind it.

'You are with me, Christine,' he said, 'Don't worry. Nothing will hurt you.'

'But what about that poor man?'

'He is in my care too,' said Marturion. He actually smiled at her – while the man in his care was drowning in the sea! Christine felt quite indignant. And yet – everything was growing lighter all around. The dark clouds were moving away from them.

'Look down,' said Marturion.

They were floating high above the sea. She saw a patch of blue appear among the grey racing waves, and realised that the sun had poked through the clouds somewhere. Then there was another blue patch and a twinkle as a wave reflected a sunbeam. Soon the whole sea was blue and sparkling. Far away she saw a little ship with a torn and dripping sail. Marturion waved his arm in its direction.

'They will make it to harbour now,' he said, 'but *we* go in this direction.'

Christine felt the breeze and the warm sun, and as she realised that she and Marturion were actually moving through the air – flying – she forgot all about the poor drowned man, and let herself be filled with the delight of it all. It was like Peter Pan, and all beautiful dreams come true. A cormorant flew past – within a foot of her – and she wondered if she were still invisible. Flying was like swimming; she found that she had stretched out her free hand (the other was still holding Marturion's) and her legs were floating along behind, pedalling gently. It wasn't even as hard work as swimming.

Now she saw below rocks and a pale yellow beach, and now they were coming down, with a pleasantly descending sensation, like the Big Wheel, thought Christine. Her legs came under her, and she landed feet first in a small sandy cove, quite empty. Little waves came lapping up to the sand, then backed away and began all over again. The sun was warm and the breeze was warm. Christine felt as if she were on holiday, and began to fancy a swim. She looked at Marturion, who was gazing out to sea, not shading his eyes against the sun. He was watching something intently. Christine stared too, shading her eyes. She saw something black, just for a moment, then it was gone. No, that was it again, a bit further out –

something long and dark. What was it? A fish?

Suddenly, further out to sea, she saw something wonderful, something she would never ever forget. Up from the water rose a great black dripping thing – a huge tail. It waved slowly to one side then flopped back into the water making a great splash. A whale's tail! Christine had seen a picture of one, with something underneath about 'its only enemy is man'. Now she had seen a real one. She turned at once to Marturion, and he was smiling and pointing. Seeing the tail was one thing; sharing the joy with someone who felt the same was even better. Marturion was not one who talked a lot but she could see he too was elated at the sight of the whale.

Christine did a whoop, and performed three cartwheels in a row on the sand to let off some steam. When she finally came upright Marturion wasn't looking and applauding as she'd hoped, he was staring out to sea again. Christine went and stood beside him and stared too, hoping to see the great tail again, or even, perhaps, the whale's spout! This time she saw a small black dot against the slope of a wave. Not a whale – it looked more like a swimmer's head. Of course it could be a seal. As the next wave rose up, there it was again, and it was definitely not a seal – she saw an arm come out of the water. Quite soon they could see the swimmer clearly. The sea was calm, the waves scarcely breaking. He came nearer and nearer and stood up at last.

He was a very strange-looking character. His skin was a peculiar white colour, and he was dressed in rags and very shaggy. Christine supposed that he must be a ship-wrecked sailor, but why was he not brown and sunburnt as sailors always are? And there was no sign of a wreck. Suddenly she remembered the storm, and the man who had fallen overboard – could it be this man? Marturion had had charge of him, he had said, and now they were waiting on the beach while the man waded ashore. But Marturion said nothing. The man did not seem to see them – at least, he did not greet them. His hair and beard were quite long and he screwed up his eyes in the sunshine – perhaps he couldn't see them properly. But he seemed to see something because he changed direction ever so slightly and came towards Marturion. As he stepped out of the water on to the dry sand he staggered, moving his lips and then threw himself down right at Marturion's feet.

Marturion bent down and touched the man on the shoulder. He said, 'Don't go to sleep, Jonah. You might change your mind. Better set off at once. There's a freshwater stream over there.'

He pointed and the man roused himself, sat up and looked. Christine looked too, and saw a little trickling stream running down among rocks on to the beach. The shaggy man jumped up and ran towards it. He took a long drink and splashed water over his thin face, sighing blissfully. Then he looked slowly all around him at the sky and the beach and began to smile. He went down on his knees facing Marturion (but Christine still didn't know if he saw him), and clasped his hands fervently together. He said, 'I'll never forget this as long as I live. I'll go now right away and do what you told me. If it costs me my life, or whatever happens – it doesn't matter any more. The Lord has rescued me!'

Then he jumped up and began to march across the beach without looking to right or left, but he marched not like a soldier, upright and stiff, but in a swinging swaying way, his half-dried rags fluttering behind him.

'How strange he is – he looks like a tramp,' thought Christine.

Then she had a sudden thought, and turned to look out to sea. Almost as she had expected, she saw far, far out to sea a spout of water. She grabbed Marturion's arm, 'Look,' she said, 'that was a whale! And did you call him Jonah?'

Marturion was laughing at her, 'Very good, Christine,' he said. 'At last! I wondered when the dawn would come.'

6

The man from the sea

They walked across the beach slowly. Jonah had already scaled the rocks that enclosed the little bay. He turned at the top, and looked back towards them for a moment. Just because he was so ragged and so wild and his face was death-coloured, he looked awe-inspiring. He turned and went over the rocks and disappeared from view.

'Where is he going?' whispered Christine.

'To the great city of Nineveh,' replied Marturion. 'He has a job to do there.'

'But why is his skin such a funny white colour?' said Christine. 'He looks like a sailor – I thought he was Sinbad the Sailor at first. He walks like a sailor, but he isn't a bit sunburnt.'

'His skin will renew itself in time,' said Marturion, 'If you'd been pickled in digestive juices for a few days, you'd lose some of your pigments, you know!'

'Gracious!' said Christine. She had heard of Jonah and the whale, but had not thought how it could actually happen.

Marturion took her hand, and they floated gently up from the beach.

'Have you enjoyed it?'

'Oh yes,' she said, looking all about her, 'in spite of the beginning – the beach was all the lovelier because of the storm. I'd like to stay here for ever,' she said, hopefully. But they rose higher and higher.

'I must show you something else before you go back,' said Marturion.

They drifted without effort, and noiselessly, through the sunny air, and Christine saw land passing beneath them – a great wide golden hilly place, with an occasional little clump of green. Evening came and the great sun sank. Deep shadows crept over the yellow land, turning it grey. Then it was night and Christine and Marturion were among the stars. She did not feel cold or sleepy, but immensely happy.

It did not seem long before they saw ahead and below them trees and white buildings with turrets and watch-towers. The sun was rising now and Christine had to shade her eyes from the dazzle. Birds were twittering riotously all around her. It seemed too glorious.

'Behold, Nineveh!' said Marturion.

'Oh, it's wonderful,' cried Christine, and immediately they began to move down. There was that lovely sinking Big Wheel sensation again, but even before they had alighted in one of the streets, Christine was aware of a very unpleasant smell. To be quite honest one would have to say that the place stank. Christine held her nose and looked about her, and then she got close to Marturion and held on tight to him with the other hand. She was dreadfully disappointed. Time must have been passing at a different rate to the one she was aware of because it was now full daylight in the city and the street was crowded with people. It was hot and dirty and there were piles of rubbish everywhere, which was what seemed to be the main cause of the smell. Close up, the houses were not so awfully white – it was only the sun's reflection on them that had given them that pristine look. But it could have been a beautiful city if it had been clean. And if it had been full of attractive people; only it was not. They were all mean-looking; Christine couldn't see a single nice face.

The children were dirty, ragged and barefoot but Christine naturally took more interest in them than in the adults. She was horrified and alarmed when she saw one little boy start to whack a donkey with a whip. The poor beast was tethered and the boy seemed to be doing it for fun. He was a good-looking boy with clear brown skin and curly black hair, but he was obviously going to become one of those hard vicious-looking men that she could see all around. No one was trying to stop his cruelty, and when Christine started forward, Marturion laid a hand on her arm and said gently, 'It is no use – for he cannot see or hear you and you cannot touch him.'

'Oh', cried Christine, 'But don't let him do that! You can stop him!'

'Yes,' said Marturion softly, 'With fire from above! With brimstone and with thunder – but I am not permitted yet. They are to have one more chance.'

'They don't deserve any chances!' cried Christine again, and this time she didn't bother to keep her voice down, but shouted loudly. No one in the market took the least bit of notice. A half-starved dog slunk by and a child sitting near a basket of oranges threw a stone and hit it in its side, whereupon it ran away with a yelp of pain. Christine was nearly in tears.

'Don't you care, Marturion?' she whispered.

'Yes, I care,' said Marturion, 'There is great wickedness in the city and you have just glimpsed one small happening. There is very much more. Oh yes, we do care.'

At that moment Christine saw a pretty girl about her

own age walking among the crowd. The girl wore a green tunic with an embroidered border, and she had a puckish, smiling face. She was throwing some shining beads up in the air and catching them. When she got near the child by the oranges, she threw the beads a little too far and they landed at the other child's feet. The child stooped for them and as he did so the puckish girl grabbed an orange and shoved it beneath her shawl under her armpit. Then she cried out and slapped the child who had picked up her beads, seized them and ran off. Shocked and fascinated, Christine stared after her. At first she had thought that the girl had looked nice – the sort she would want for a friend. Then she realised that she had had a sly look in spite of her prettiness. She knew Marturion was looking at her and she turned to him. He was very serious, even sad.

'Are you sad about that girl?' she asked. 'I suppose she's not worse than the rest of them.' And even as she spoke, she remembered the girl putting the orange under her armpit to hide it and she saw herself in the cloakroom at school with the ball. Then her face blushed red with shame and she turned away from Marturion, thinking that he was rather an uncomfortable friend to have.

Just then they heard a voice some way off. They could hear it even through the din of the market-place.

'Perhaps they have Town Criers here,' thought Christine, as the owner of the voice came into view. People in the crowd stood back and made way for him. They fell silent and the man who was calling out came and stood right in the centre of the market-place. He had a rolling sailor's walk and a powerful, bawling sailor's voice and it was Jonah.

He was saying, 'Repent – turn from your evil! Thus says the Lord. Turn to me and I will save your city. Otherwise, if you continue in your evil ways I will bring destruction on you. This is certain and nothing can change it.'

Then he began to tell them his story. He had been sent from the land of the Hebrews, he said, and given this message for Nineveh. But he had refused to do it, at first – he had taken ship at Joppa and gone in the opposite direction. Then, he went on, a terrible storm had come upon the ship. He described the storm in detail and made everybody's blood run cold. They had thrown the cargo overboard but it became clear that nothing could save the ship. Then they had all started calling on the gods to save them, all except Jonah who knew it was no use him speaking to God when he had disobeyed him. Then the sailors had drawn lots to find out if anyone had brought ill-luck upon the ship.

Jonah paused dramatically.

'I drew the short straw,' he said finally. The people in the market-place sighed all together like a gust of wind. Jonah looked around. 'I told the other sailors to throw me into the sea. Only by my death was there any hope that the ship might be saved.'

There was now an icy stillness about the crowd and Christine felt the fear as everyone stared at Jonah, hardly daring to breathe or move. Then Jonah smiled, and his face lit up.

'No, I am not a ghost,' he said, and again there was a great sigh, this time of relief.

'But I have come back from the dead just the same,' said Jonah. 'Look at me.' Christine saw the people freeze once again, still rapt and amazed as Jonah described his next experience.

'I saw a greater darkness than the darkness all around, and I was swept into it, with the seas about me, but the turbulence of the waters died down and I found I was in a great cave and there was no daylight at all. I clung on to the sides of the cave and the waters came up and down beside me. It was completely black but I felt as though I were rushing downwards at great speed. I thought I was dizzy from lack of air, but there *was* air, though it was foul, – I *was* able to breathe.

'I was in that cave for so long that I gave up all hope. Sometimes I felt that I was falling into the depths of the earth, and my head was squeezed so hard, I wondered that I had not died at once. Then I thought, "I am in hell – I have died, and dying is not peace and rest or nothingness, it is this terrible loneliness and blackness."

'It was then that I called upon the Lord of heaven and earth. I remembered why I was in this dreadful place. I repented that I had not obeyed him and I told him that if he would deliver me from this terrible hole that I had fallen into I would serve him again as I had vowed to do. Then I had peace and I rested. I must have slept and loosed my hold upon the sides of the cave, for I awoke and found myself in water which was flowing and taking me with it. Then I saw daylight. I put all my strength into swimming towards it. I swam out of the cave and I was in a calm sea – the sun was shining and there was land ahead. Then I had hope and I began to swim towards it with all my strength. But I saw something dark in the water beneath me. I looked and there was a huge fish diving. I saw its great tail rise out of the water, and if it had come towards me I would have been drowned – it was tall as a ship's mast! Then its tail slapped the water with a mighty splash that made great waves and I swam like a madman towards the land – my fear gave me strength.

'But when I reached the land I fell down and

worshipped my God who made land and sea, and it was then I knew that I had been in the body of that fish – there had been no cave, and the movement I had felt had been the fish diving.'

Jonah raised his staff and brandished it, 'This is why I tell you to repent and turn to follow the true God – the one who made heaven and earth – for he is able to do anything and in a short time Nineveh will be overthrown. The Lord has spoken it. You must turn from worshipping idols and doing evil in the name of the gods! Go upon your knees. Wear sackcloth and fast. Obey the Lord for it will surely come to pass. I have come from the dead to tell you.'

He turned and strode from the market place, and all the people followed him. They were awed and terrified and amazed. Some were weeping, some covered their heads, some took hold of their cloaks and tore them. Christine watched them, just as amazed at their behaviour. When the market-place was emptied, and the stalls abandoned to the stray dogs, Christine stared around her, and turned to Marturion, 'Imagine the people of London – or Manchester – tearing their clothes like that!'

'Your people are surfeited with wonders – the wonders of technology, that is. They do not care to know any others – or do they?'

'Some do. *I* do anyway,' said Christine, and he gave her a friendly smile.

Then nodding in a satisfied way after Jonah, he said, 'He is going to walk right through the city now – from one side to the other, telling his message. So *we* will go on.'

As she took his hand, immediately she was in a different place. But it was quiet and peaceful, so she was able to get her breath back. They were on a high hill and she could see the lovely white city spread out below them. (But she felt differently about it now that she had been inside.)

'Soon it will be beautiful inside as well as from afar,' said Marturion, reading her thoughts again, 'Look once more, Christine, and remember it.'

There was something Christine felt she wanted to ask Marturion, but it wouldn't come into her mind. As she looked down at Nineveh its towers and buildings were glowing peach-coloured in the evening sun. She became dazzled by the glow in the sky, but as she turned back towards her friend, everything began to vanish away. And though she tried and tried to hold on to it, as you do to a wonderful dream, – it went – and soon she was sitting on the floor of her room, surrounded by all the things she had pulled out from under her bed, and with the little blue-grey box in her lap.

For a few minutes she sat there still, wishing she could get back to the hill above Nineveh. She could still hear Marturion's voice. 'He has such a beautiful voice, 'she thought, 'But any rate I can write down the things I remember him saying.'

Then it seemed to her that she had better put away the seventeen books and the dirty socks, and when she had done this, her mother came and knocked on the door.

'You're very quiet,' she said.

'I was tidying my room,' said Christine proudly.

Mrs. David gazed round at what still seemed a shambolic mess. Then she spotted that the bed had been made. Determined to look on the bright side, she said, 'The bed looks nice.'

'And under it!' said Christine, pleased, 'The bit you can't see is really clear now. I've got ever so many books from under there. And tomorrow I'm going to tidy my chest of drawers.'

7

The girl in the lovely house

The next day Christine went to the dust-bins and found the ball lurking behind one of them. She put it in her pocket and went up to Joanna. 'Here's your ball,' she said, getting it out and handing it over. 'I did hide it yesterday, and I wish I hadn't.' She was amazed at herself, being able to say this. She nearly added, 'I'm not going to get spiteful like you lot,' but realised in time that it sounded priggish, so she stopped.

Joanna took the ball silently, and Christine didn't know what she was thinking, but at any rate, she herself felt so much better that she didn't care what Joanna thought. She ran into school, and while she was taking off her coat she watched Lara and Fiona wrangling together in the corner. She wondered what it was about Lara that made the others all follow her lead. It couldn't be her looks – she was rather plain. She was a good runner, of course. But she was so bossy and domineering. Christine wondered if Lara had her own way at home, if she had always had her own way, if the other children had followed her lead from their first day at school? She had a devoted follower in Fiona, even though they quarrelled from time to time. The two of them made a strong team.

Christine thought Fiona was a pretty girl. She had a round face and dark curly hair. But she seemed to have no ideas of her own, and just followed Lara around like a little pet dog. She puzzled about this while she changed her shoes. Joanna came and sat on the bench beside her.

'I know!' said Christine, thinking aloud.

'What?' said Joanna. Christine turned and looked at her.

'You know the story of Snow White? And you know the wicked Queen?'

'Yes?'

'Well she was the most beautiful person in the world, wasn't she – until Snow White grew up. I've always wondered how she could be so beautiful when she was so wicked. It doesn't seem right.'

'Ah, but in the end she turns into an ugly old woman,' said Joanna,' I saw the film last year with my little sister.'

'Oh have you got a little sister? So have I!'

'I've got two,' said Joanna, 'and two older brothers.'

'That must be nice – you're never stuck for someone to play with.'

'No, I suppose not. But it gets so noisy!'

In the classroom, Lara was handing out invitation cards in an ostentatious manner, to all the girls.

'Here you are, Joanna,' she called out loudly, pushing past Christine, 'it's an invitation to my party.' She glanced at Christine out of the sides of her eyes, 'Now let's see – who hasn't had one?'

She shuffled through the little pile on her desk, the girls all crowding round her.

'Where's Mandy? Not here yet? Caroline?' Her voice was loud enough but she raised it still more, 'Susie! Here you are! Now there's just Caroline and Mandy to come. Any more? No that's all.'

She glanced round at Christine who was burrowing into

her desk, hoping not to be left out, but afraid to look too anxious. Lara began to describe the party.

'We're going to have a buffet tea, and afterwards fireworks in the garden, and a bonfire. My father owns a toy-shop and he's going to bring all the left-over fireworks from November 5th.'

'Who's coming altogether?' asked somebody, and Lara reeled the names off in a loud voice. Sally and Julie were not on the list but that didn't bother them. Christine pretended not be bothered either, looking for something in her desk. She heard Joanna's voice say, 'What about Christine?'

'Oh no!' said the voice, clear and malicious, '*She*'s not coming. We don't want *her*!'

They all went off then to play netball in the hall, but Christine remained behind the lid of her desk, swallowing back her tears. She still went through the motions of looking for something, though everything was blurred. Her fingers touched some soft material, and she blinked her eyes hard. The little shoe-bag came into focus. The Eye of Time and Space? She didn't remember bringing it to school this morning, nor putting it in her desk. Marturion had said it would help her. But how was it helping her? She fingered the little bag in a depressed way. What use was going into the past? It didn't alter the future or the present, except to make you forget your troubles for a time.

She sat, full of self-pity, almost enjoying being sorry for herself. Then without her trying, the memory of Marturion began to push itself into her mind. Lara's loud spite began to recede, and her friend's voice came faintly back. Now, more than anything, she wanted to be with Marturion again. And so far Marturion had always been with her whenever she had used the Eye of Time and Space. She opened the bag and took out the box.

It was gold. It had changed again. She stared at it breathlessly. It seemed like pure gold, bright and heavy in her hands. She glanced over her shoulder, then quickly back at the box afraid that it might disappear. But it was still there so she opened the lid. Even as she did so the box grew enormous and she saw a flight of stone steps opening out in front of her. They gleamed white and Christine saw a paved stone courtyard at the bottom and a pool with a little fountain splashing. Large-leaved plants and brilliant flowers were growing around it. All was sunny and quiet. Christine crept nervously down the steps. She put her hand on a stone balustrade. There was a carved creature with wings at the bottom and just as Christine got to it she heard running footsteps and instinctively crouched behind the winged carving.

There were white buildings all around the courtyard and through an archway in one of them a girl of about her own age came running. She had bare brown arms and shoulders and a white tunic with a border in a brownish-red pattern. She looked all around as if she were running from someone and didn't know where to go next, and Christine saw her face twisted and twitching as if she were fighting tears. Then she threw herself on to the ground beneath a plant with dark green leaves, and began to sob heart-breakingly. Christine sympathised with her at once. Only a short while ago that had been just what she had felt like doing. She wondered what this girl could have to cry about – she seemed to be living in a lovely house. Christine felt she would like to be wearing a tunic like that and to have long black hair that spread all around on the ground the way the girl's did. Then she saw Marturion standing beside the girl. She had not seen him come. Although she felt delighted to see her friend again, Christine also knew a stab of jealousy because Marturion was looking down at the other girl. But it was only the merest twinge – the next second he was looking at her and beckoning.

'Come along,' he called. 'She can't see or hear you.'

Christine stepped on tiptoe from behind the carving and walked stealthily up to him. He laughed, and then she began to laugh and she was so full of joy again that she forgot the miserable girl on the ground. Then Marturion looked down and Christine remembered.

'Who is she?' she whispered, 'Why is she crying? Is there anything I can do?'

'You can feel for her,' said Marturion, 'She's a long way from her home and she's lost both her parents. She was taken prisoner in a raid and now she's a slave in this house. It's a Syrian house,' he added.

'Oh!' said Christine, and stopped feeling the slightest bit envious of the girl, 'I was thinking this was her home,' she said, looking all around at the pleasant white walls. 'But what happened to her parents?'

Marturion looked seriously at her.

'She doesn't know – she thinks they may be dead. And possibly all her little brothers and sisters too. She was the eldest.'

Christine was going to persist, 'But *are* they dead?' Something in his look made her stop. Instead she faltered, 'But how awful. How can people do things like that?'

'Oh,' said Marturion, 'they are always doing such things. And worse things. They do such things in your time too – people haven't changed.'

Christine was going to reply indignantly, when he said,

'You have newspapers – television – radio – you hear what is done every day. Is it so hard for you, Christine, to believe how wicked people are?'

'No,' said Christine, and she remembered the children at school.

'But take heart,' said Marturion, '*You* aren't so very badly off – and neither is this girl.'

They both looked at her again. She was just lying there sniffing.

'You were right in a way – she has a lovely house to live in, she has enough to eat, and a kind master and mistress. But she's like you, Christine – lonely. You two could be friends – '

'Oh yes!' cried Christine enthusiastically.

But Marturion said, '*but* you cannot reach each other – you are in a different time. You will both have to make do with me.'

Christine leaned down, determined to touch the girl and see what would happen. But her fingers touched what seemed to be a glass wall. She could not get through to the girl no matter how she scrabbled at it. After trying and struggling for a bit she pulled a face – Marturion was sitting cross-legged on the ground laughing at her. No, he wasn't quite touching the ground – it was just as if he were in another place which was superimposed on the one the girl was in. Christine sat beside him – she wasn't quite sure if she were sitting on the same ground as he was or not. She certainly felt as if she were sitting on the ground.

'Well, what are you going to do?' she said to Marturion.

'I may not be seen by her, but I can give her thoughts and ideas. We can carry on a conversation, listen.'

The girl was sitting up now, drooping one hand in the

little pool. Marturion leaned slightly towards her and spoke.

'You are here for a purpose,' he said softly. 'You escaped death in the raid – there is a reason why you are here.'

'What can be the purpose of anything,' said the girl in a dreary voice. 'I've got no one left now – ' She began to sniff again.

'You mustn't spend the time being sorry for yourself,' said Marturion. 'You must keep alert, be on the look-out. You have something to give these people even though they've been enemies to you.' His words were bracing but his voice was kind. 'You have been brought up to believe in the one true God. *They* only know about their idols – they learn ugliness from the demons who inhabit their bits of wood. You could help them.'

'I know,' said the girl, 'But they won't listen to me – they don't want to learn anything better – '

'The opportunity will come,' said Marturion. 'You must be ready. Don't hide away like a snail in a shell. Wait for your chance and it will come. I will help you.'

The girl brightened up a little and stood up smoothing down her tunic.

'Well, I will try,' she murmured, then, hearing a voice in the distance, she hurried away back through the arch.

'Would you like to see inside this house?' Marturion asked Christine, and they walked together up the steps she had come down. At the top, instead of the school classroom, there was a door, and there were latticed windows in the wall above the courtyard. They went through the door (without opening it) and Christine caught her breath with excitement for it seemed to dissolve all around her as she went through. Yet when she looked back over her shoulder there was the door, solid as ever.

Her eyes had to get used to the light inside the room for the courtyard had been very bright. The brightness came through the latticed windows and made tiny patches like diamonds, but the rest of the room seemed dark.

Christine could hear voices and gradually she made out a man and a woman sitting together on a couch covered with the most beautiful rugs and cushions. The man was dressed in a linen robe with an ornamental chain around his neck and an embroidered band round his head. He put his arm towards the woman with a look of suffering on his face and she reached out and gently turned back the sleeve of his robe. Christine thought, 'Oh he's been wounded' for he looked like a soldier. And then she saw what the woman was looking at. It was a plain white patch showing up on the sunburnt skin, dead and white-looking.

'It's no bigger, I'm sure it's no bigger,' the woman said. She had a sweet sympathetic face.

'It's a matter of time – we know that,' replied the man gloomily. He put back the sleeve to cover the patch and held both the hands of the woman and they were quiet, not looking at each other for a minute or two.

'I must go to the king, my dear,' he said.

He kissed the woman, and stood up. She got up too and laid her face against his shoulder for a minute. He went out. Christine watched him and when she turned back to look at the woman, she saw that she was on her knees beside the couch, with her face buried in her arms, and her shoulders shaking.

'Oh dear,' whispered Christine, 'This is a sad house. What a pity. It should be happy – it's such a lovely place.'

Marturion just smiled; he looked joyful and excited.

What a strange person he is, she thought. He seems to be so happy he can't keep it in. It makes me happy just being with him, and he never says, 'Cheer up' the way some people do – and make you feel worse! I feel he knows such a lot more than I do. He knows there's nothing to be unhappy about, I suppose.

The sad woman in the lovely house did not know this, of course, though she was now getting up and wiping her eyes. When a servant came in and salaamed, the woman spoke without looking at her. 'We will spin today, Ruth. I must be busy. Go and fetch the other maids.' As the servant was going out of the door, she added, 'And fetch the little Hebrew girl too. I'd like to know what sort of child she is, and what she can do.'

The maid salaamed again and went out, and soon various women came in and took distaffs from a beautifully carved chest in the corner. The first maid, Ruth, came back, followed by the girl Christine had seen crying, carrying between them a great basket full of fleeces. They put it down on the floor and the maids settled themselves around it, and began to spin the fleece, the mistress of the house working too. But she asked the girl her name, and the girl replied, 'Sarah'.

After they had been spinning a while (Christine was very interested in watching them do it), the mistress of the house told Sarah that she was doing very well, and that if she were neat and obedient she would train her to be a maid and companion to her own daughter. Sarah began to look much more cheerful at this.

Christine now had time to have a good look round the room. She was surprised at its bareness, no pictures on the walls, no flowers in pots or vases, no bookshelves full of books. On the other hand, the carvings on the low tables and on the chest, were such as she had never seen before, not even in antique shops, and the coloured rugs and cushions made a glow against the white walls. She pictured her own room at home – the litter of papers, pencils, felt-tips and things.

'It does make it much tidier,' she thought, 'if you don't have reading and writing things about.' She supposed that in this age only a few people could read and write, and paper (or would it be papyrus?) would not be all that plentiful. She wondered if the women spent all their days spinning or doing needlework. She thought she would like to have a go at spinning but she didn't think she would like to spend all day at it.

8

The man in the river

Marturion touched Christine on the shoulder and she followed him back through the dissolving door and up more steps on to a flat roof. From there she could see all around – there were trees and fields around the house, and other houses in the distance. Across the courtyard a group of children came running. They stopped and turned round as the handsome man she had first seen came out of a room on the ground floor and strode across towards what seemed to be the main gate. He walked with a swing with his head up, and he now wore a cloak and had a dagger in his belt and was accompanied by a servant. He stopped and talked to the children for a moment and ruffled the hair of one and picked up another, a little girl, high in the air, and waved her about, laughing. Then he put her down and waved goodbye gaily enough, though when he turned back towards the gate, Christine could see how sad his face had now become.

When he had gone she wandered about on the roof and watched the children playing together. She saw the kitchen area and watched a servant grinding corn with a stone. She noticed again that time seemed to be passing differently from the time she was in. Quite soon she saw that the sun was lower in the sky and that people were returning to the house from the fields. A meal was being got ready. Marturion showed her a room where the mistress was saying goodnight to the children, and Sarah was standing behind her fanning her with a fan that was bigger than herself.

At last the children's nurse took them out and the woman was left with Ruth, who began to do her hair, and Sarah, who kept on fanning. Her mistress seemed to have forgotten Sarah, and she said to Ruth, 'If only there were something that we could do! Day after day I wake with a great weight on me.'

The maid said, 'Perhaps, my lady, it will get no worse. Perhaps a healer will be found. Perhaps Rimmon will heal him.'

'Rimmon!' said the woman, in a voice of despair, 'We must face facts. There is no cure. It will get worse. One day my husband will have to resign his command – the king knows it, and we know it. I feel I can't go on sometimes.' And she gave a deep sigh.

'We must try to live one day at a time, Madam,' said Ruth, also sighing. They were silent for a moment then her mistress said, 'See if all is ready for the meal, Ruth,' and the maid bowed and went out.

All this time Sarah had been standing fanning with an intense expression on her face, as if she'd thought of something. She was like someone who is dying to answer a question in school, but is not given a chance. Suddenly Marturion spoke. Christine heard his bell-like voice clearly in the room, as Ruth shut the door behind her.

'Now,' he said, 'your chance is coming, Sarah. Make the most of it.'

Sarah was biting her lips anxiously and Christine heard a little voice in her head which said, anxiously, 'I am not supposed to speak unless my lady speaks first. If I offend her that's the end of my chance to speak.'

Marturion just smiled at Sarah. The woman spoke in the silence.

'Are you happy here, Sarah?'

Sarah was astonished and said, 'Well, Madam – I – '

'I saw you crying this morning – down by the fountain. You are lonely, I expect. Tell me about your home and your country.'

Sarah took a deep breath and said, 'Damascus is a beautiful city, my lady. My city – the city of Samaria – cannot compare with it. But, my lady, we have something in Israel that you do not know about. Oh, my lady,' she burst out, 'If only my lord Naaman could visit the prophet we have in Israel, he would heal him of his leprosy, surely. The prophet who is in Israel performs miracles, my lady, in the name of the living God. If my lord would go to see him, surely he would be healed. He brought a little boy back to life once, my lady – the family lived near us.'

'A little boy back to life? Are you certain? Tell me more about it!'

'It is true, my lady,' said Sarah eagerly, 'Everyone in our district was talking of it. The little boy had sunstroke and died. His mother went to fetch the prophet herself, and when the prophet came to the house he shut himself in the room where the boy was. And after some time he brought the boy out alive.'

Her mistress sat up, excitedly. She looked quite feverish.

'Go to my lord's room and tell his servant that I would speak with my lord as soon as he returns! We will find this prophet. We'll try anything!'

Sarah ran from the room, overjoyed, while her mistress walked up and down by the window, up and down, up and down, clasping and unclasping her hands, and biting her lips nervously.

Marturion turned to Christine, 'Now,' he said, 'We will go and see what happens to the great soldier, Naaman the Syrian.'

He took Christine's hand, and she found herself rising up, and then she and Marturion flew over the countryside. Presently they began to come lower, and she could make out the land more clearly. There was a thick dark-green forested area, then she made out a glint of water, and a little later she saw that this was a winding river.

They came swooping in very low now, almost brushing the trees, and dipped even lower over the water. Christine saw that they were coming towards a clearing at the riverside, where a group of men stood. Quite a lot of time must have passed. One of the men was Naaman – a cross and frowning Naaman – another was the servant who had gone out with him through the gate when he had gone to the king.

Marturion and Christine landed on the shore quite near enough to the group to hear what they were saying. As usual no one took any notice of them, but by now Christine was so used to this that she took it for granted. She concentrated, and heard Naaman saying, 'To tell me to bathe in this muddy little river! Can he *really* be a prophet? I expected him to do a magic spell! I wouldn't have minded a really nasty one – anything to make me better! He didn't even bother to examine the spot! He must be an impostor.'

One of the men said, 'But my lord, it's worth a try. After all he has a tremendous reputation in Israel, apparently.'

'I find that hard to believe,' said Naaman petulantly.

'Funny-looking fellow.'

Another servant said, 'But sir, it's not a difficult thing to do.'

'I know! That's just it – dip in the Jordan seven times,' said Naaman, derisively. 'It's an insult. It was deliberate cheek. There are plenty of rivers in Syria – much better ones.'

'Just so, my lord, but it's not worth going back without doing it, is it?' said the third man persuasively. 'You said yourself, if it'd been something hard or nasty you'd have done it without flinching. Just to take an easy swim, do a bit of diving – it can't hurt, you might as well. . . .'

Naaman looked as if he was considering this.

'Go on, sir, give it a try,' urged the others.

(He's very popular with his men, thought Christine.)

'It might even work!' said one. Naaman grinned then and took off his cloak, then his tunic. He shrugged his shoulders and ran into the water. He threw himself headlong and submerged. Then he came up and floated on his back. They could all see the white spot on his arm quite clearly. 'One,' said all the men, and Marturion and Christine, together. Naaman plunged under the water again.

'Two,' said the men on the bank.

He did it again. 'Three,' they said. Still the white patch showed. Down he went again, again, again. He dived under for the last time. He seemed to stay under longer.

'Seven,' said all the men, as his head broke the surface.

Naaman stood up and waded out of the water. He stopped and looked at his bare arm. His brown skin shone in the sun. He looked at the other arm. The men all ran down into the water and crowded round him. They were all looking and peering at both his arms. Christine couldn't see. And they were so silent. She wanted to say, 'Stand back a bit – do let me see the spot.'

Suddenly the silence was broken. Naaman burst into tears! And the men began hugging one another, like footballers that have scored a goal. They began hugging Naaman, and he hugged them back, with tears running down his face. Now at last Christine could see both his arms and they were quite brown and there was nothing to be seen on either of them.

Marturion was beaming. He took Christine's hand again and raised his other arm and they soared up into the air like two birds, but when they had passed over the slopes that bordered the river, Christine saw a clearing before some rocks and a stone house. In front of it, on the ground, sat a stocky man. He had not much hair and a pleasant round face, sunburnt and healthy with twinkling brown eyes. He was smiling contentedly and gazing into space. As they came nearer he looked right up at Marturion and nodded in greeting. Marturion said, 'What's wrong with the Jordan after all?'

And the little man roared with laughter.

They flew on. Christine was thinking all this over.

'Marturion,' she said timidly, 'Was that – could that have been – that jolly man, I mean – he wasn't the prophet, was he? The one Naaman went to see to be healed?'

'Elisha,' said Marturion, 'Yes, that was old Elisha – great fellow!'

'He's quite different from Jonah, isn't he?' said Christine, 'Jonah – he *looked* like a prophet. But Elisha – he – he looks like my uncle!'

'And why shouldn't he?' laughed Marturion, 'Just think – anyone – anyone can let my Lord – the Living God

– use them! And we're all different! How glorious to be part of it all!'

His voice and his laughter were all around in the air like music, like echoes of music. . . .

Christine was sitting at her desk, listening to the echoes. She sat there with the golden box in her hand for some time. There was something so happy about Marturion that it was catching – the way a fire warms everything around it. She felt warm and happy. Then the classroom door burst open, and she hurriedly pushed the box into the bag as the others came stampeding in.

9

The Prize

It was after lunch. Christine leant against a wall in the pale wintry sun, idly bouncing a ball she had brought to school. She didn't even try to join in with the others. She didn't ask. She thought, 'I've had enough of being snubbed.' She found she didn't mind being alone any more. When the bell went for the beginning of afternoon school, she saw Joanna hurrying in through the gate. Christine didn't rush to join the line – she just started to stroll across, planning not to be standing anywhere near Lara. Joanna came towards her.

'Christine!' she called out, so Christine waited.

'I've asked my mother,' said Joanna, 'and she says yes, so will you come to tea with me on Saturday?'

Christine was really astonished and she could only stare for a minute. The temptation came into her head to say no, rudely, and hurt Joanna's feelings. Fortunately, she remembered in time that she had promised herself not to get spiteful. So she said, 'I'd like to very much, thank you.' And then remembered something else and her heart sank to her boots with the old disappointment.

'Oh no! It's Lara's birthday party on Saturday!'

Joanna looked interested. 'Oh, have you had an invitation?'

'Oh no!' said Christine, 'Not *me*!' (She couldn't help

sounding a bit sarcastic.) 'But *you're* going, aren't you?'

'No,' said Joanna, 'I don't want to.'

'Why not?' asked Christine, who loved parties.

'Oh, I don't know,' said Joanna in an off-hand manner. 'Well, I do *really*. See, I don't like Lara much, and I think she's mean not to invite you, and anyway I shouldn't like her sort of party.' She held out the reply card that had come with the invitation. She had filled in the negative reply.

'I'm just going to give it to her. Coming?'

Christine followed her, quite dumb.

Lara said, 'Oh what a shame! Why can't you come?'

'I'm doing something else,' said Joanna calmly.

Lara was quite sympathetic.

'Oh, you poor thing! Have you got to go somewhere with your mum?'

'No,' said Joanna, 'But I'm having Christine to my house for tea.'

Lara pulled a frightful face.

'Oh, that's even worse! Poor you! Put her off! Tell her you're invited to my party.'

Christine stared open-mouthed at Lara's rudeness in front of her. But Joanna did not seem at all ruffled. She only said, 'I don't want to go to a party. I'd rather have Christine to tea with me.' She turned away to her desk.

Lara had a very nasty look in her eye.

'I hope you enjoy yourselves!' she said sarcastically.

'I wouldn't want *her* in my house,' said Fiona.

Christine was nettled, 'Well that's all right, because I wouldn't want to come.'

Joanna said nothing. She was getting out her Bible and notebook because this was the afternoon Mr. Roberts the curate, was coming. Christine really admired her just then. She saw Joanna with new eyes. Up till then she hadn't thought much of her because she was quiet and easy-going and had seemed to go along with the crowd. Christine had thought that she was weak and couldn't think for herself. Now she saw that Joanna had taken her time, and had made up her mind for herself, and now that it was made up, nobody's persuasion, or scorn or jeers would make her change it. How often she'd longed for just one member of the class to stand on her side against Lara and the rest. And now it had come – but not at all as she would have imagined it. No shouting, no declaiming, no slapping of Lara. Joanna, the quietest one in the class had just firmly rejected Lara and was now ignoring her as if she were not even there.

Mr. Roberts came in with a folder in which were the stories the class had written the week before. He put it on the desk and took a huge bar of milk chocolate from a paper bag, and laid it on the desk beside them. Everyone's mouth started to water. Mr. Roberts went on and on in the most maddening way, instead of coming straight to the point and saying who had won the chocolate. He read out little bits from various stories, not saying whose they were, or whether any of them was the winner. He held up some of the pictures that had accompanied the stories. He praised the work a great deal. At last he got to the matter of the prize.

'The story I've chosen,' he said, 'didn't have any pictures, but it was such a good story, so well described, that you could see the pictures in your mind.'

Christine's heart missed a beat. She had been so busy writing that she had not time for pictures. But then, others could have done the same. . . .

'This story,' went on Mr. Roberts, 'made me think the

writer had *been* there!'

Everyone laughed. Except Christine. She waited in breathless suspense.

'The story was written by Christine David. Come on, Christine – come and get your chocolate!'

She got up, and went out to the front, glowing, beaming and red-faced. Mr. Roberts began to clap. Christine heard everyone joining in. She stood there at the front. This was the first time she had felt part of the class.

'Now she's going to read it to us,' said Mr. Roberts, as the clapping died away.

Christine was a very good reader, and when she had finished reading the story out, everyone clapped again, quite spontaneously this time, without Mr. Roberts starting them off, and they turned to look as she went back to her seat. There were friendly smiles and one or two of the boys clapped her on the back. She felt so happy, the misery of the morning – being left out of Lara's party invitations – just faded away. But while she was sitting there in a glow, it came to her that she had had an advantage which was definitely unfair. Mr. Roberts had been right when he had said that he felt as if the writer had *been* there, because she had! And of course it had helped her write the story. She wondered what he would say if she went and told him this. She had *seen* Joseph, she had seen his brothers, she had seen the traders who had bought him. She would have to show the Eye of Time and Space to prove it though. But of course she couldn't do that, because it was a secret! Marturion had been very serious and emphatic about that in the beginning. One thing was certain – she was not going to do anything to hurt or offend him.

I don't see what I can do, she thought, staring hungrily

at the bar of chocolate. Then a solution came to her – she could share the chocolate out between everyone in the class. That was something at any rate.

At break everyone crowded round her, and they were all nice.

'How did you write it like that, Christine? It was really good!'

'It was just like a book!'

'It was better than mine – look that's all *I* wrote!'

'You deserved the prize.'

Christine unwrapped the chocolate and began to count the squares. There were twenty-four squares – it was just right. She began to break it up and give them out. The children were not surprised that she should do this, though they probably wouldn't have done it themselves. They thanked her, and went out to the playground, chewing. In the end there were just three squares left – Christine's own one, and Lara's and Fiona's. A voice said inside, 'Don't give them any – they're not your friends.'

But another voice said, 'That's got nothing to do with it. The chocolate belongs to the whole class. You didn't win it fairly, so it's not just a matter of giving it to your friends.' Christine had a battle, especially as Lara and Fiona hadn't come up to her to congratulate her, and seemed to be nowhere around to claim their shares. However, justice prevailed and she put the last three pieces, one on each of their desks, and one in her mouth. Then she went out into the play ground, bouncing her ball.

Almost at once several girls crowded around her saying, 'Can I play?'

This was something new. Christine threw the ball to Joanna. She knew now, what she hadn't thought of before, that it didn't matter whether she was popular with the class or not. All she needed was a real friend, someone who would stand by her. She would play with Joanna – and if the others wanted to join in, all right, they could. They did. They turned themselves into two teams somehow, and raced about laughing and jumping. The bell went – it had seemed a very short break. They crowded into the line, panting, and queued up at the drinking water tap in the cloakroom.

'Everything's changed,' thought Christine. 'I wonder why.'

Lara and Fiona were already in the classroom.

'What are you doing here?' asked Mandy.

'Mrs. Andrews said we could tidy the sewing cupboard, so there!' said Fiona, pulling a face. They both looked slightly furtive, over there by the cupboards pushing scissors into a box. Christine wondered if it was because of the chocolate she had put on their desks, but neither of them said a word of thanks. That was the only nasty thing about that afternoon; she wished she hadn't had to give them a piece of chocolate. Everyone else had been nice to her. Still honour had been satisfied. The rest of the afternoon went by peacefully.

When hometime came, Christine remembered the Eye of Time and Space that had been in her desk that morning when she had needed it. But now it was not there – she searched the desk twice. At last she jumbled everything back into it in a heap and went into the cloakroom to look under her coat. She thought she had put it back in her desk, but as she scarcely ever remembered where she had put things, she was not too worried. But it was not under her coat. Now she began to worry. She *had* had it in school, hadn't she? The last of the children were going out of the classroom, and her mother would be waiting with Anne. She ran back to the classroom and met Mrs. Andrews who was just coming out, and told her that she had lost a shoe-bag. Mrs. Andrews said, 'Now Christine – stop and think for a minute. Remember where you were when you had it last. Try to think where you put it down. Try to imagine yourself holding it – you're good at imagining things, aren't you? If you start thinking like that, other things will come back to you.'

Christine sat down on the nearest chair and shut her eyes. She remembered sitting in the classroom with the gold box in her hands listening to the echo of Marturion's voice, feeling warm and happy, and it didn't matter any more that the others had treated her like an outcast. Then she remembered them all bursting in from playing netball in the hall, and she had quickly stuffed the box into the bag and into her desk. And she had not had it since. Well, that was it. It *must* be in her desk.

She opened her desk, and two thoughts came to her.

One was that she had not remembered bringing the bag to school that morning. Could it be that it had power to move itself?

The other – much more disturbing – was that Lara and Fiona had been on their own in the classroom during the afternoon break. What if they had caught a glimpse of the golden box in her hands that morning? Would Lara really be dishonest enough to take it from her desk?

She searched the desk for the third time. It was not there.

'Are you sure you brought it to school, Christine?' asked Mrs. Andrews, coming back, 'Don't you think you'd better go home and look? Was it something special?'

'Yes,' said Christine, afraid she might let out the secret

of the bag, 'But I may not have brought it to school – I'll have to go home now anyway, so I'll look there.'

'That's right,' said Mrs. Andrews, 'I hope you find it, but if not, come and tell me again in the morning and we'll ask the class if anyone's seen it.'

10

The lost box

It was not at home. Christine looked absolutely everywhere she could think of. She longed to ask her mother to help her – (her mother had the gift of finding things that other people had lost, she had noticed) but she knew she must not tell the secret of the bag. Before she got into bed that night she prayed.

'Oh God,' she said, 'you must know how worried I am. You know I feel desperate because I've lost it. Please help me find it. Please, please, please'. . . . She could say no more. She got into bed with a sort of peace because there was no more to do and no more to be said. She fell asleep.

When she awoke it was greyish light and it was morning. She could hear her father moving about downstairs making coffee. She lay there with a great sense of peace and happiness and she knew she had had a dream which had brought her a wonderful feeling. She closed her eyes and tried to bring it back, but there was not much that she could remember, only that she had been with Marturion in her dream and he had said something – what was it? He had been in the classroom and all the other children were there and they could see him too! It had been marvellous. Then the words that he had said came back, 'Till the end of the world,' he had said. 'For ever and ever.'

Christine hugged the happiness to her – even when the memory of the loss of the bag came back to her.

'Maybe this dream was given to comfort me,' she thought, 'So I'll try not to think about the bag. Maybe I'll just find it accidentally, and it'll have been quite safe all the time.'

She decided not to go and tell Mrs. Andrews she had not yet found it. Morning school began and after they had done their Arithmetic, everyone got busy on their projects. It was drizzling so they would have to fill in their time indoors unless it cleared up. About half-way through the morning a paper dart landed on Christine's desk. She could tell by the way it was pointing that it had come from the boys' side. She looked across. Ian was pointing at the dart and making 'Open it' signs with his hands. Christine laughed at him at first but he seemed very urgent and quite serious, so she unfolded the paper.

'Lara has your shoe-bag.'

That was what it said. She stared at it. Dismay, misery, hopelessness all swept her down with them. She looked back at Ian. He was nodding at her vigorously. Just then Mrs. Andrews got up from her chair and Ian went back to his work.

Now Christine was in a quandary. She couldn't work any more; that was certain. The butterfly book lay open before her with the note on top of it, and the horrid words burning into her mind. Should she rush out to Mrs. Andrews and wave the note at her and demand that Lara's desk be searched? But it was Ian who had told. How did he know anything about it? He'd got into trouble the other week for fighting Lara. She thought she'd better ask him first, so she wrote on the note, 'Shall I tell Mrs. Andrews?' folded it and flew it back.

It seemed an age before he finally looked her way and shook his head emphatically.

'Why not,' she thought angrily, wishing she hadn't asked him. Why did the boys have to be so silly about not telling the teachers anything? Still, she couldn't very well tell now – and she hadn't even got the note for proof. She sat there while the morning dragged on. The class was in a quiet working mood that morning and they all decided not to have a morning break but to finish school twenty minutes earlier instead. Mrs. Andrews brought her coffee into the classroom and everyone carried on with their project work. Everyone except Christine. She didn't even try to get interested in her butterflies again. She turned the pages of the book listlessly, . . . she had finished off Vanessids and now she had to start the Fritillaries. They were so complicated, so difficult to draw. Whatever would she do about the Eye of Time and Space? Could Ian have been making it up? But no, he didn't know she'd lost anything, so he must have seen Lara with it. How could he have known it belonged to Christine? And how was she to get it back from Lara? . . . 'Orange brown butterflies with dark spots' – better write that down, Mrs. Andrews was coming round looking. . . . Should she face Lara with the truth? And would Ian back her up? What if Lara denied knowing anything about it? And oh – what if – what if she had looked inside the bag? . . .

The headmaster, Mr. Haviland, came into the room, and everyone looked up expectantly while he talked to Mrs. Andrews in a low voice and gave her a piece of paper.

Mrs. Andrews looked at it and then said to the class, 'In a few minutes I shall tell you to pack up, but meanwhile carry on with your work – all except these people – you are to go to Mr. Haviland in the hall.' Several hands shot up to volunteer, but Mrs. Andrews ignored them and read from a list in her hand. Christine was scarcely listening, engrossed with the idea that morning school was finishing and that she must get the Eye of Time and Space from Lara somehow. . . .

'Christine David.'

Oh bother – her name was one of the four read out. What could Mr. Haviland want them for? At any other time she would have been pleased.

But when she got to the hall she nearly forgot her worries, because she found she had been chosen to be one of the readers at the school Carol Service which would be taking place next week. Christine was given the passage from the book of the prophet Isaiah, which begins,

'The people who walked in darkness have seen a great light;

Those who dwelt in a land of deep darkness, on them has the light shined.'

It goes on to describe the Prince that would be given to the land of Israel, and ends with the words,

'With justice and with righteousness from this time forth and for evermore. The zeal of the Lord of Hosts will do this.'

Christine had always loved the beauty and the poetry of that passage, hearing it read out in Church year after year at Christmas time, but this time the last two lines brought back her dream, and she saw in her mind's eye her friend Marturion standing among the children in the classroom and saying the words, 'Till the end of the world. For ever and ever.'

Although she did not know at all what it meant, it lifted her spirits.

After they had had a practice and had been told to go

over it at home, they were free to go back to the classroom, or out to the playground, as the rain had eased off. There were only five minutes left now before lunch-time and the other three hurried to the cloakroom to wash their hands and be first in the lunch queue. Christine went to the classroom.

As she opened the door, she saw that the room was empty except for a little group of five – Ian and the twins, with Lara and Fiona in the middle. They all looked up at her as she came in, almost as if they had been talking about her.

Lara was holding the shoe-bag.

Ian said, self-importantly, rather enjoying himself, 'That's it. Now you'll cop it!'

After the first moment of shock, rage boiled up and over in Christine.

'Give me that! That's mine! You rotten thief – you stole that from my desk!'

She threw herself around and across the desks. If only she could get the bag back before Lara opened it. . . .

'Now then – what's this?' said a voice behind her. Mr. Scott, the Class B teacher had come out of his room next door. Christine paused, two desks between her and Lara – in all her anger and relief and distress she had noticed how yellow and strange Lara's face was. . . .

'Sir – she took something of mine – make her give it back! She's got my bag.'

'Sure it's yours? Has it got your name in it?'

'No, but it is mine, sir, she got it out of my desk. Ian – tell him,' she said desperately, thinking that Mr. Scott would not take the matter seriously.

'It *is* her shoe-bag, sir,' said Ian, to her great relief.

'It isn't a shoe-bag!' said Lara viciously, 'and it's only

got rubbish in it – I don't see what all the fuss is about. Look!'

Even as Christine screamed and tried to reach and snatch the bag and prevent it from being opened; even as the rest of the class came pouring into the room; even as the lunch bell rang – Lara jerked the bag open, held it up and tipped it upside down. The Eye of Time and Space fell out on to the desk in front of everyone.

'Silly little cry-baby – take your old bit of tin!' said Lara, and stalked out of the room, throwing the bag over her shoulder on to the floor. Fiona looked curiously at Christine's face, and followed Lara.

Christine stared dumbly at what lay on the desk, while all the other children crowded round to look. The box – the beautiful box. It was the same size and shape – but now it seemed to be made of tin – battered, rusty old tin. Not pure gold any more. Christine picked it up and cradled it in her hands. Sobs rose up in her throat. Her tears fell on it.

'Well, there you are,' said Mr. Scott, turning to go, not noticing that she was crying, 'Everything all right now. Off you go, everyone – lunch-time!'

'Yes, sir,' they said, but when he had gone they crowded closer.

'What is it, Christine?'

'What have you got?'

'What are you crying about?'

'Nothing – it's gone – it's spoilt – or she's changed it!' cried Christine beginning to blaze with anger again.

'She took that tin out of your bag, if that's what you mean,' said Ian, 'I was in here so I know.'

Christine stared at him.

'You know this morning I saw her over by the sewing

cupboard before the others came in, and I saw her with that bag – it was in the cupboard, and she looked at it and she said to Fiona, "she hasn't found it yet". Then I knew it must be your bag that you put into your desk yesterday – I'd seen you putting it in your desk yesterday. . . . There wasn't time to tell you before Mrs. Andrews came in. Then when you had to go to the hall, I thought I'd get the bag for you, but when everyone had gone out Lara and Fiona stayed behind, so I got down behind a desk and watched them.'

Ian's dark eyes were twinkling – he loved an audience.

'They got the bag out of the cupboard,' he went on, 'And Lara said "Now we'll have a look" and she put her hand in and said "What's this?" and she got out that tin you're holding now. And then she opened it!'

'She opened it!' Christine's despair was complete. She felt that faith with Marturion had now been completely broken and she would never see him again. She clutched the rusty tin to her chest, both hands covering it.

'What happened?' she said in a hoarse, dull whisper. She felt she knew the answer – 'Nothing.'

But Ian said, 'I couldn't see her hands or the box because I was behind this desk, but she made a queer noise – it was like she was choking – I think it gave her an electric shock – she went all yellow and her eyes were popping out – and I jumped up and saw her throwing it back into the bag. Then *you* came in (he nodded at the twins) – and the next minute Christine comes in – so there you are. Is it something electrical?' he added curiously.

Joanna had picked up the bag and handed it to Christine. She put the little tin inside.

'No – I don't know – it's something I was given. No one was to touch it.'

'Why did you bring it to school?' asked Nicola, accusingly.

'I – don't know – it was a mistake.' It was all Christine could think of.

'I'm going to lunch.'

She took the bag along to the cloakroom, while the other children wandered along to the lunch queue. Once again she hid it under her coat and went back to the hall. She got in the lunch queue. Her mind was on anything but food. It was a confusion of ideas, and the noisy dining-hall was the last place to think things out. She wished she were at home.

Lara was not in the dining-hall, and that afternoon she was not in school. Fiona, when asked, said that she had had to go home because she felt sick. She gave Christine a sideways glance, as she said it, so that Christine felt it was all *her* fault.

When Christine finally got home, she went up to her bedroom and put the box in its bag on the shelf at the back of the wardrobe, where she had decided to keep it when she had tidied her room. She did not want to look at it again – it had been such a shock to see it, such a poor thing, so despoiled. It had become dangerous too. Whatever had it done to Lara? And yet, she wanted to keep it safe, to protect it almost. It was dear to her, for what it had been – like an old dog that has become ugly and tired, perhaps a little cross, but you love him just the same, maybe more. Still she could not bear to look at the box as it was now. It would be a long, long time before she took it out again. . . .

11

The last adventure

She awoke in the night – someone was shaking her. No, she was lying quite still in bed in the dark. That is, it was dark outside the window, but light somewhere else – was there a light on somewhere in the house? She turned over on her other side, and there was Marturion beside the bed, with that soft light about him, that she had seen in the storm.

'Oh!' she cried, with that feeling you get when you wake up and know it's your birthday, 'Oh – you're here – and you've come without me opening the – ' she faltered and her sadness returned as she remembered what she had to tell him.

Marturion actually sat down (or seemed to) on her bed and gave her his joyful smile, 'I have been here all the time,' he said, 'I was beside you in school. Don't you understand, Christine? I am the one who has charge of you.'

'Oh yes,' she said, feeling more cheerful though she never did know what he meant when he said that. But if he knew what had happened, why wasn't he angry?

'Do you know what Lara did to the Eye of Time and Space?' she said.

He nodded. Then he patted her arm.

'She can't hurt it, you know. It hurt *her* – but *she* can't do anything to *it*.'

'Oh but she has! She's ruined it, Marturion – she's made it ugly and old and sort of used-up. . . .'

'No, Christine – it changes – it does not remain the same – you know that.'

'Do you mean – that the next time I took it out it would have looked like – like *that* – after it had been gold. . . .?'

'No, I do not mean that. The Eye of Time and Space changes according to *who* picks it up, and why – '

'Oh,' she paused – she felt so relieved, so very relieved. 'It was like *that* for Lara then.'

'Forgive her, Christine.'

'How can I ever forgive her,' Christine burst out at once. 'She's the most awful girl. She's the one who led all the others and kept me out of everything. She *made* them not like me. I don't know why she hates me. I've never done anything to her. But I hate *her* now – and I've got reason to.'

'Yes,' said Marturion, 'But if you hate, you are poisoning *yourself*. You don't want to do that, do you?'

'Of course not,' she cried, 'but I can't help hating her.'

Marturion said, 'Then we had better take another journey together. This time, I will show you my Lord. He can take hate away for you.'

Christine shrank back. She had often noticed Marturion mention his 'Lord', and she had secretly made a guess as to who Marturion was. He was not just a space-man, or an extra-terrestrial being. He was someone from outside Space and Time. And if he was that, then surely the only one who could be his Lord must be God himself. And how could she Christine, possibly see God? Unless she died first. . . . 'Oh no, Marturion,' she stammered, really frightened, 'I couldn't, I just couldn't. I don't dare.'

'Don't be afraid, Christine. We can use the Eye of Time and Space. We will go, and return, together,' said Marturion.

She looked into his happy face, and all her confidence rushed back. She took a deep breath, 'Well, all right. But *you* must hold it.'

Marturion reached into the wardrobe and took out the bag, then removed the box. It was gleaming silver as he took it out – the lid was engraved with a pattern and decorated with gems like emeralds. It was restored! Christine was so glad that tears came into her eyes again and she instinctively held out her hands. Marturion put the box into them and Christine lifted the lid.

This time inside all was summer blue and the blue spread until it was all around them. Then they were standing on a high mountain and it was lovely just being there and seeing the earth spread around below, green and gold, brown with touches and flashes of blue. Little fluffy clouds passed along just below and somewhere they could hear a skylark.

After a moment or two, though, Marturion said, 'Now we must go down,' and they both stepped off the mountain top into the air like a couple of swimmers stepping into a pool – this time Christine was quite confident about it. They floated slowly down, mountains and hills rising up around them with rocks and grass, then here and there a little flock of grazing sheep, and it was all beautifully quiet, except for the skylarks. Once they passed very near a hawk, and once a large bird shot past, going down. Christine wondered if it were an eagle.

They were coming towards a little valley among the hills which was full of colour. As they drew nearer, Christine could see that the valley was crowded with people, who covered the floor and the steeply-sloping sides and who all seemed to be watching and listening to something. It looked like an outdoor theatre to Christine, who had once been to the Minnack Theatre in Cornwall. Only here nobody had thermos flasks and rugs, like the people in the Minnack. Instead they shielded their heads from the blazing sun with pieces of material which hung to their shoulders; and some had leather bottles slung over their shoulders. They were all listening to a man who sat on a rock, about where the stage would be, telling stories.

The acoustics were good – you could hear his voice clearly all around the valley. Once again, as Christine watched him, she found that she could understand what he was saying. He was telling a story about a wonderful party. A rich man was giving it, and there was to be everything good there. He described the rich man giving the orders, organising everything – he acted the voices. Then came the giving of the invitations; these were sent out to all the people he knew. But – to the astonishment of the servants, the invited guests began to make excuses. The story-teller acted their voices and the things they said were so silly that his audience all laughed a lot – some laughed till the tears rolled down their faces. Christine laughed because the others were laughing and because the man made it sound funny, but she had an idea that all the people around understood the joke better than she did.

Then the speaker's voice changed and he became serious and rather sad. He talked about the rich man's feelings when he found that the guests he had invited were not interested in his party.

He told how the rich man lost his patience and sent his servants out around the town to look for all the poor people and the beggars and lay-abouts. He described the servants bringing them all in through the gates of the rich man's house, and the people smiled again at some of his descriptions. But this time they only smiled rather ruefully, as if he had made some point that was just a bit painful.

Yet when the story came to an end and the story-teller took a swig from a water bottle, the people all began to clamour for more. They roared and cheered and the sound rolled round the valley like thunder.

The young man took a long drink. Then he passed the water bottle back to one of his friends who stood near him, and began to talk again. He started to talk about a woman who had lost something very precious – it was a gold piece out of her necklace – and it was the most valuable thing she had. She told everyone about it and then she began a thorough search of her house. The way he told the story was so dramatic, there was a hush in the valley – the woman took a broom and swept up every bit of dust and rubbish from every corner of her room. Christine felt as if he must have been there that time she had got everything out from under her bed (only this woman did not have dirty socks and seventeen books among her rubbish). In other respects the story was so similar to her own that she felt he might have been speaking just to her – he described her feelings so exactly when she had lost the Eye of Time and Space.

And then the woman found the gold piece! A sigh swept around the valley – the audience was living the story as well as Christine. What joy there was! The man described the woman running into her neighbour's house to tell her, laughing, nearly crying. He pictured her and her friends having a party to celebrate. Everyone in the valley was smiling.

'It's just like that in the Kingdom of Heaven,' said the young man. 'Joy and rejoicing over just one person who is brought back into the family of God.'

Christine looked at Marturion suddenly. All this time – however long it had been – the story-teller had been so interesting she had almost forgotten that she was not in her own time and that Marturion had told her he would take her to see his Lord. Marturion was radiant and proud.

'So Christine,' he said softly, 'Now what do you think of Jesus?'

'Jesus?' she was so startled that her eyes opened wide, and something made her afraid to look anywhere but at Marturion, in case the whole valley, and the story-teller on the rock, should just fade away as she looked at them. She stared hard at Marturion's face.

'That's not – is it? – ' she was so afraid she was making a mistake.

'Don't worry, Christine – we will not go away just for a little while. You may look again – do look. I brought you here to see him.'

Christine looked almost fearfully. There he was. She had always thought of Jesus as being so remote – kind and good, but far away – not at all like this vivid, lively person just a few yards away, sitting on a rock. Somebody was going up to him – somebody with a limp. One of the group who were standing around talking cheerfully, reached out a hand and helped the limping woman nearer. Jesus spoke to her, he looked concerned. Then he laid his hands upon her head. Christine saw the woman turn round with an uncertain look on her face – she took a few steps as if feeling her way – then her walk became stronger, more certain. Her face brightened and she went back to her friends, not limping any more, while all the people nearby who had seen it, cheered. Now more and more people began to make their way up to the rock. Christine said, hopefully, 'Oh, I wish *I* could go up and talk to him – just talk to him – could I, do you think?'

'No, Christine, you cannot do that now – because we are not in Space and Time, remember? My Lord has come down into it, and just for a little while he is part of it. But you are an onlooker, and *I* can only enter it to help those I have charge of. But look – here is one of my charges!'

He pointed to a boy who was, like Christine, watching the crowds around Jesus with a wistful look on his face. He was with a crowd of other boys, but while they were all chattering and talking and larking about, now that the story-teller had come to an end, this boy seemed to have something on his mind. Christine felt that he was like her – he looked as if he would really love to go and speak to Jesus. But Jesus was healing people now; and there was nothing wrong with the boy. He began to edge nearer, however, and Marturion walked beside him. Christine went along too.

They all got as near as they could, and time went on, and the three of them waited patiently. Now and again Christine caught a glimpse of Jesus between the heads of the crowd round him, and each time she saw him he looked more weary, more drained of energy. A long line of sick people moved up to him and away. At last there were no more people needing healing, and Jesus' friends made a barrier round him and glared off-puttingly at all the healthy people who were waiting about, just hoping for a personal word with their master.

Marturion now tapped the boy on the shoulder. 'Maybe he's hungry – don't you think he could do with something to eat?' he whispered. The boy started, then peered into a bag he was carrying. He then looked about at Jesus' friends, and picked the one with the kindliest face. This was a big man with crinkly eyes. When the boy went up to him, he bent down and listened with a friendly smile, as if he liked youngsters. Christine heard the boy say, 'Would Jesus like something to eat?'

The man said, 'That's kind of you, lad. What've you got?'

'Well – ' he dug into the bag and got the things out, 'this is all I've got left, but he can have it – five loaves, and two fishes – small ones. Will it be enough, do you think?'

'Let's see,' said the man. He put one arm around the boy's shoulders and took him into the group around Jesus. Marturion and Christine kept close behind.

Jesus had been saying something as the group opened to let the big man and the boy join it. It was as if they were interrupting something. The big man said, 'There's a lad here with five loaves and two small fishes – any use?'

What really surprised Christine was the way Jesus and his friends suddenly began to laugh and several of them clapped their hands, just as if the two had made an entrance at a funny moment. Jesus held out his hand to the boy in a welcoming way, even as he laughed. It was a rich happy sound. Christine saw his dark eyes glowing, and for a moment they flickered past the boy as if they saw her too.

Marturion said, 'He was just suggesting that they feed the people – all five thousand of them – '

Christine began to laugh too, 'Of course – then that boy came along!' Then an idea dawned upon her, '*You* sent him along just then! I heard you – '

She looked at her friend in amazement, feeling quite as confused as the boy with the loaves and fishes must have done. Marturion was laughing.

'We like jokes you know – it was our side that invented them. The Enemy doesn't understand what they are really.'

Christine thought that when she got home she would write that down. She looked back towards Jesus. He was talking earnestly to the boy. She felt really envious – she could hear his voice, but there was no translation – it was all in a foreign language, just for the boy alone. She saw the boy nodding eagerly, then he handed over his little dinner bundle. Jesus took it and unwrapped it and placed in on the rock in front of him, as on a table. The boy sat down on the grass beside him, and then Jesus held his hands over the bread and blessed it and prayed a prayer of thanksgiving.

And then Christine watched the miracle. She saw his hands breaking the bread, and putting a piece down on the rock and breaking the other piece, and giving it away, and there was always bread on the rock before him. His friends took the pieces away and gave them to the people, she supposed, but she kept her eyes on the fine, strong, brown hands, breaking the bread, and breaking the bread.

Then there were the little fishes, broken and broken again, and always a little piece of fish lay on the rock before him. Until after a long time, the friends were eating, and the boy was eating, and then at last, Jesus was eating, and all around him there was a silence, and beyond the pool of silence, there was a quiet murmuring in the valley like bees going home to bed.

Jesus's friends had been eating the food cautiously as if afraid that it might not taste right. Then they changed their expressions, as if it tasted far better than they had expected! But they still remained silent, as if under a spell.

Jesus looked about the group.

'Friends' he said, 'see if you can get some baskets and collect up any bits that are left over – we could use them up tomorrow!' They went off very willingly, the boy with them, as if only too glad to be able to do something.

Marturion held out his hand to Christine.

'Well – we must go now.'

'I wish I could have joined in,' said Christine.

'One day you may yet,' said Marturion, 'There is still plenty of time. You will find him in the future as well as the past.'

They moved up into the air, climbing, as if on invisible steps. Christine had done this, sometimes, in dreams. It had always been delightful, but now she went reluctantly, still looking down at the solitary figure stretched out on the grass behind the rock, then on the colourful valley full of going-home sounds. Then the high mountains hid it from sight.

They floated over the mountains, and came a little lower over a shimmering lake set in the hills, and lower still and further on, they came to a city, golden in the setting sun.

'Look just once at Jerusalem,' said Marturion.

Just once – and while she was still looking, it was there no longer, and she was looking into the little golden box. Its lining had been the colour of the golden city, but it was now fading, fading to palest cream.

It was cold now, and it was dark – she was sitting here on her own bed, in the middle of a winter's night with the central heating off. But Marturion was still there. She looked up at him, and grew cold inside when she saw that his hand was held out. Even his happy face looked regretful. She knew without needing to be told that the time had come to give him back the Eye of Time and Space

– it had only been lent to her at the beginning. She closed its lid gently and looked down at the lovely shining silver and the deep gleaming emeralds. She felt tears coming into her eyes and wondered if she should let them drip on to the box. Maybe Marturion would change his mind, if he saw tears.

'It is not my mind,' said Marturion, 'I am commanded and I obey. I am only a servant – would you make things hard for me?'

She felt very ashamed then, and looked down at the box again.

'Christine, I am still with you. Do you know that now? Do you understand?'

'Yes, Marturion, but it's not the same. It won't be the same if I can't see you, and if we can't travel about together.'

'No, but one day it will be better, and you will see me again. And meanwhile you have a job to do.'

'*I* have?' she had heard him say that before to other people, several times – but now it was to *her*.

'Yes, Christine – you too. Gradually you will understand what it is, and one day you will be able to look back and see how it all worked out. And I am always your friend remember, and my Master is your friend.'

Christine took a deep breath. 'Well,' she said slowly, 'you are my very great friend, Marturion, and I'll never forget you – what you look like, I mean. And I'll never forget the places we've been to, or anything. And I'll try to realise that you're still here when I can't see you.'

He was smiling at her now, as if pleased with what she had said.

'Here's the box, then,' she said, putting it firmly into his hand, 'and thank you, thank you, thank you for everything.'

She got into bed and settled herself on her side. Then she thought of something. 'Could you stay here – I mean, so I can see you, just while I go to sleep? Then in the morning I expect it won't be so bad.'

'I will stay here,' he said.

She closed her eyes, meaning to open them again to take another peep, but when she opened them it was morning, a dreary, dark, winter's morning – she could hear her father rattling the cups in the kitchen. Marturion was not to be seen. And the Eye of Time and Space had gone. However, Christine was bursting with energy and happiness! She did not stop to try and work out why, but rolled out of bed and ran straight into Anne's room next door. Her little sister lay in bed with one hand under her flushed cheek, and her fair hair tangled over the pillow. Christine stared, thinking how beautiful she was – like a little angel. She spoke the little angel's name.

'Anne!'

The dark lashes flicked up immediately and Anne smiled at her at once, as if pleased to be awakened!

'Hallo Kissy,' she said, rolling out of bed immediately, just as Christine had done, 'Let's see who can stand on their head the longest. Till Daddy comes up, anyway!'

So that was what they did.